JOURNAL FOR THE STUDY OF THE OLD TESTAMENT
SUPPLEMENT SERIES
128

JSOT Press
Sheffield

BIBLICAL SOUND AND SENSE

Poetic Sound Patterns in Proverbs 10–29

Thomas P. McCreesh, OP

Journal for the Study of the Old Testament
Supplement Series 128

To the memory of my father,
and to my mother

Observe, my son, your father's precept,
and do not forsake your mother's instruction;
bind them on your heart always (Prov. 6.20-21).

Published by JSOT Press
JSOT Press is an imprint of
Sheffield Academic Press Ltd
The University of Sheffield
343 Fulwood Road
Sheffield S10 3BP
England

Typeset by Sheffield Academic Press
and
Printed on acid-free paper in Great Britain
by Billing & Sons Ltd
Worcester

British Library Cataloguing in Publication Data

McCreesh, Thomas P.
Biblical sound and sense: poetic sound patterns in
Proverbs 10–29.—(Journal for the study of the Old
Testament. Supplement series. ISSN 0309-0787; 128)
I. Title II. Series
223.706

ISBN 1-85075-326-1

CONTENTS

Preface	7
Abbreviations	8
Chapter 1 INTRODUCTION	11
Chapter 2 BASIC SOUND PATTERNS	24
Chapter 3 LINKING SOUND PATTERNS	51
Chapter 4 CORRELATION	64
Chapter 5 TAGGING SOUND PATTERNS (1)	75
Chapter 6 TAGGING SOUND PATTERNS (2)	
1. Coordinating Proverbs	89
2. Proverbs Using Imagery	106
Chapter 7 WORDS AND SOUNDS	119
1. Word Repetition	120
2. Repetition of Word Roots	142
3. Wordplay	149
SUMMARY	154

Bibliography 156
Index of Biblical References 161
Index of Authors 163

PREFACE

This represents a limited revision of a doctoral dissertation that was submitted to the Department of Semitic and Egyptian Languages of The Catholic University of America in Washington, DC in 1981. Its purpose is to show that the study of sound patterns is an integral part of the investigation of OT Hebrew poetry. Such study, although a normal part of poetic criticism in general, has not received enough attention with respect to OT poetry, because either its sound patterns were thought to be too few and insignificant or its analysis to be too complex. Besides answering these criticisms by an extensive analysis of some ninety sayings from Proverbs, the examples gathered here also demonstrate techniques for analysis, drawn from modern literary criticism, which could be utilized in related studies.

My interest in this subject was first awakened by Patrick W. Skehan (1909–1980) and then developed further under the direction of Aloysius Fitzgerald, FSC, both of The Catholic University of America. From the same faculty Professors Richard M. Frank and John S. Kselman, SS, helped refine ideas and guide the final stages of writing. Special thanks must be given to John P. McIntyre, SJ, who gave very helpful suggestions for the revision process, and to Mark S. Smith for his unflagging encouragement for this publication project. With special gratitude I acknowledge the support and encouragement of my Dominican family, which enabled me to carry on the studies that bore fruit in this research. Finally, I wish to thank David J.A. Clines and Philip R. Davies of Sheffield Academic Press for their interest and support, and the editors and staff of the Press for their patience as we prepared the work for publication back and forth over an ocean!

Thomas P. McCreesh, OP
Washington, DC
July 1991

ABBREVIATIONS

AB	Anchor Bible
absol.	absolute
act.	active
adj.	adjective
ANET	J.B. Pritchard (ed.), *Ancient Near Eastern Texts* (Princeton, NJ: Princeton University Press, 3rd edn, 1978)
ATD	Das Alte Testament Deutsch
BASOR	*Bulletin of the American Schools of Oriental Research*
BDB	F. Brown, S.R. Driver, and C.A. Briggs, *Hebrew and English Lexicon of the Old Testament* (Oxford: Clarendon Press, repr., 1968)
BeO	*Bibbia e oriente*
BHK	R. Kittel (ed.), *Biblia hebraica* (Stuttgart: Württembergische Bibelanstalt, 1966)
BHS	K. Elliger and W. Rudolph (eds.), *Biblia hebraica stuttgartensia* (Stuttgart: Deutsche Bibelstiftung, 1967–77)
Bib	*Biblica*
BibOr	Biblica et orientalia
BZAW	Beihefte zur *ZAW*
gen.	genitive
GKC	E. Kautzsch (ed.), *Gesenius' Hebrew Grammar* (trans. A.E. Cowley; Oxford: Clarendon Press, 2nd edn, 1910)
HALAT	W. Baumgartner, *et al.*, *Hebräisches und aramäisches Lexikon zum Alten Testament* (4 vols. to date; Leiden: Brill, 1967–)
HAT	Handbuch zum Alten Testament
ICC	International Critical Commentary
imper.	imperative
inf.	infinitive
Int	*Interpretation*
JBL	*Journal of Biblical Literature*
K.	*k^e^tîb*
LUÅ	Lunds universitets årsskrift
NAB	*New American Bible*
obj.	object
part.	participle
pass.	passive
pl.	plural
pred.	predicate
prep.	preposition

pron.	pronoun
Q.	*q*^{e}*rê*
RSV	*Revised Standard Version*
SB	Sources bibliques
SBLDS	Society of Biblical Literature Dissertation Series
sing.	singular
subj.	subject
UF	*Ugarit-Forschungen*
Ug.	Ugaritic
v.	verb
VD	*Verbum domini*
VT	*Vetus Testamentum*
VTSup	Vetus Testamentum, Supplements
WMANT	Wissenschaftliche Monographien zum Alten und Neuen Testament
ZAW	*Zeitschrift für die alttestamentliche Wissenschaft*

Chapter 1

INTRODUCTION

I

Growing interest in the literary analysis of the Bible and the ever-increasing attention given to the wisdom literature of the Bible have converged in this century on the sayings of Proverbs. In the early part of this century G. Boström[1] began studying the poetic devices of alliteration, assonance, rhyme, and other phonic effects in those sayings, a concern that does not seem to have been given much emphasis before Boström's work. A few years after Boström, W. Zimmerli[2] studied the different forms of the wisdom sentence as revealed in Proverbs and Qoheleth in order to shed light on the nature of OT wisdom, the questions it posed and the solutions it sought. In the same vein and closer to the present are the works of U. Skladny, H.-J. Hermisson and W. McKane[3] which also investigated the literary structures of the sayings, this time for clues as to their origin and history. These studies began to ask pertinent questions about the nature of proverbial language and the differences between it and other kinds of biblical language such as narrative prose or the poetry of the prophetic writings and the Psalms.

Within the last thirty years or so the whole field of OT poetry received great scrutiny, as witnessed by the mass of literature on the

1. G. Boström, *Paranomasi i den äldre hebreiska Maschallitteraturen mid särskild Hänsyn till Proverbia* (LUÅ, ns, 1.23, 8; Lund: Gleerup, 1928).

2. W. Zimmerli, 'Zur Struktur der alttestamentlichen Weisheit', *ZAW* 51 (1953), pp. 177-204.

3. U. Skladny, *Die ältesten Spruchsammlungen in Israel* (Göttingen: Vandenhoeck & Ruprecht, 1962); H.-J. Hermisson, *Studien zur israelitischen Spruchweisheit* (WMANT, 28; Neukirchen–Vluyn: Neukirchener Verlag, 1968); W. McKane, *Proverbs: A New Approach* (London: SCM Press, 1970).

subject which has been printed during that time. More recently, T. Collins, A.M. Cooper and M. O'Connor[1] have dealt with the basic question of the forms of the Hebrew poetic line. And, closer to the particular concerns of this investigation, A. Berlin's book on biblical parallelism devoted a chapter to consonance in parallel word pairs.[2] It is to this widening study of the poetry of the Bible (with special emphasis on the sayings of Proverbs) that the present investigation hopes to make a modest contribution. Therefore, the first section of this chapter will present reasons for the choice of a study of sound patterns in particular, and for the choice of Proverbs 10–29 as the text. The next section will give the arguments defending the very possibility of studying sound patterns in a dead language such as biblical Hebrew.

The narrowing of the literary focus of this volume to the study of poetic sound patterns can be readily explained. It is simply this: such a prominent feature of poetry, which even the most superficial of investigations shows to be thoroughly characteristic of Hebrew poetry in general, has not received sufficient attention in the past. Alliteration, assonance and rhyme are as native to poetry in any circumstances—early or late, primitive or refined—as are the use of imagery and other poetic devices.[3] In fact, a poetic function in language can be a very natural thing, as one critic describes in this conversation:

> A girl used to talk about 'the horrible Harry'. 'Why horrible?' 'Because I hate him.' 'But why not *dreadful, terrible, frightful, disgusting*?' 'I don't know why, but *horrible* fits him better.' Without realizing it, she clung to the poetic device of paronomasia.[4]

1. T. Collins, *Line-Forms in Hebrew Poetry: A Grammatical Approach to the Stylistic Study of the Hebrew Prophets* (Studia Pohl; Series Maior, 7; Rome: Biblical Institute Press, 1979); A.M. Cooper, *Biblical Poetics: A Linguistic Approach* (Missoula, MT: Scholars Press, 1979); M. O'Connor, *Hebrew Verse Structure* (Winona Lake, IN: Eisenbrauns, 1979).
2. A. Berlin, *The Dynamics of Biblical Parallelism* (Bloomington, IN: Indiana University Press, 1985).
3. D.I. Masson, 'Sound in Poetry', in *Princeton Encyclopedia of Poetry and Prose* (ed. A. Preminger; Princeton, NJ: Princeton University Press, 1965), p. 784.
4. R. Jakobson, 'Closing Statement: Linguistics and Poetics', in *Style in Language* (ed. T.A. Sebeok; Cambridge, MA: MIT Press, 1975), p. 357.

The political slogan 'I like Ike' is another demonstration of the natural appeal of poetic sound patterns in language.[1]

Secondly, despite the renewed interest in the literary analysis of the Bible, the sound patterns of the Hebrew poetry in the OT have not been given enough attention. The poetic sayings in Proverbs have been only occasionally noted in studies primarily concerned with other things. Apart from this, there are, besides Boström's, just two works worthy of special mention: I.M. Casanowicz's pioneering study of the device of paronomasia and the third chapter of L. Alonso Schökel's major work on Hebrew poetry.[2] The characteristic point of view which largely prevailed concerning sound patterns in Hebrew is aptly summed up by C.H. Toy in his book on Proverbs:

> there are. . . occasional assonances or rhymes; but these are of irregular occurrence, and obviously do not belong to the essence of the form of the verse.[3]

This investigation hopes to show that the only thing such an attitude reveals is that the whole matter of sound patterns has not been seriously considered.

Thirdly, the lack of such an awareness of these poetic devices of sound increases the likelihood of sometimes misunderstanding or even correcting the Hebrew text. For example, the word *wāzār*, though of uncertain meaning in Prov. 21.8, should likely be allowed to stand because of its clear alliterative link with the following word *w^{e}zak*.[4] The sound patterning in this proverb, in other words, provides a basis for retaining the MT as it is and not deleting or correcting a troublesome text. A solution to the meaning of Prov. 21.8 will have to be found in other ways. In Prov. 15.24 the words *lm'lh* and *mṭh* have caused considerable debate over their meaning in the context of that particular saying. But when they are viewed against the background of the /l, ma/ sound pattern throughout the proverb there is little

1. Jakobsen, 'Closing Statement', p. 357.
2. I.M. Casanowicz, *Paronomasia in the Old Testament* (Boston: Norwood, 1894); L. Alonso Schökel, *Estudios de poética hebrea* (Barcelona: Juan Flors, 1963).
3. C.H. Toy, *A Critical and Exegetical Commentary on the Book of Proverbs* (ICC; Edinburgh: T. & T. Clark, 1970), p. viii.
4. For a fuller discussion, see Chapter 3.

question that those words belong there.[1] Such suggested changes betray the unfortunate fact that, for the modern investigator of the OT, Hebrew words are largely signs to be seen, not words to be heard. An awareness of sound patterning in Hebrew poetry can help avoid such hasty emendations while providing, at the same time, important auxiliary arguments for such tasks as textual criticism. In addition, the analyses presented here, which have been developed on the basis of more sophisticated systems of phonic[2] analysis employed in the study of contemporary poetry, will have the advantage of being models for analysing other bodies of poetry found in the OT.

The choice of the sayings in Proverbs as the basic text for analysis was not simply a matter of building on work already done, nor was it just the case that Proverbs could supply more examples of poetic sound patterns than other OT books. There are some practical reasons for the choice. The first is that the proverbs provide the researcher with short, manageable units which make possible a more complete analysis than could be the case with longer pieces. Longer poems generally present numerous side issues which can only distract from the task at hand. Another reason is provided by the current interest in proverbial language as an important speech form in both the OT and the NT.[3] Any study of even just one aspect of proverbial language (such as sound patterns) will help further this research.

A third reason for studying the sayings of Proverbs can be found in the very nature of proverbs themselves. Among other characteristics,

1. For a fuller discussion, see Chapter 4.

2. 'Phonic', a generic term, is really used in this study for 'phonemic', as will become clear in the following analyses. See L. Bloomfield, *Language* (Chicago: University of Chicago Press, repr., 1984), pp. 78-82; also H.A. Gleason, Jr, *Linguistics and English Grammar* (New York: Holt, Rinehart and Winston, 1965), pp. 104, 109, 421. Although I do not use standard phonemic notation, I do use the convention of enclosing sequences of letters between slanting strokes to indicate sound patterns.

3. Some examples of this interest are provided by R.E. Murphy, 'The Kerygma of the Book of Proverbs', *Int 20* (1966), pp. 3-14; W.A. Beardslee, 'Uses of the Proverb in the Synoptic Gospels', *Int* 24 (1970), pp. 61-73, and his *Literary Criticism of the New Testament* (Philadelphia: Fortress Press, 1970); J.M. Thompson, *The Form and Function of Proverbs in Ancient Israel* (The Hague: Mouton, 1974); T.R. Hobbs, 'Some Proverbial Reflections in the Book of Jeremiah', *ZAW* 91 (1979), pp. 62-72; and C.E. Carlston, 'Proverbs, Maxims and the Historical Jesus', *JBL* 99 (1980), pp. 87-105.

proverbs in all languages manifest a heavy incidence of sound patterning. The Italian saying 'Oro non fa odore' is formed around the repeated use of the /o/ vowel. The consonants /l/ and /g/ are the prominent sounds in 'All that glitters is not gold'. In the Latin saying 'Praemonitus, praemunitus' the difference of sound between each word is crucial but involves only the switch of an /o/ vowel to /u/. The sound pattern in the English version 'Forewarned, forearmed' involves only two changes: the dropping of the /w/ and the change of /n/ to /m/.[1] Proverbs from even older cultures are not lacking in sound patterns, as this example from the Mari archives illustrates:[2]

šuppatam išātum ikkalma u tappātaša iqullā.
š   t m š t m
š pp t   t pp t š
*   ikk l   iq ll*

Wherever proverbs are to be found, there is a close connection between the content of a proverb and the way it is expressed.

This is even reflected in different definitions of the proverb. The humorous ones, such as that attributed to Lord Russell, 'The wisdom of many, the wit of one', or the definition derived from M. de Cervantes, 'Short sentences drawn from long experience',[3]

1. The example is found in A. Taylor, *The Proverb* (Cambridge, MA: Harvard University Press, 1931), p. 144.

2. 'Fire consumes a bulrush and its companions pay attention', from *Archives royales de Mari*. X. *Correspondance féminine* (ed. G. Dossin and A. Finet; Paris: Librairie Orientaliste Paul Geuthner, 1978), No. 150 ll. 9-11.

3. Both are quoted by A. Dundes, 'On the Structure of the Proverb', *Proverbium* 25 (1975), p. 971. Lord John Russell's remark about proverbs was actually, 'One man's wit and all men's wisdom'—as reported to Sir James Mackintosh in a conversation on October 6, 1830 and recorded in *Memoirs of the Life of the Right Honourable Sir James Mackintosh* (ed. R.J. Mackintosh; 2 vols.; London: Edward Moxon, 2nd edn, 1836), II, p. 473. M. de Cervantes' actual phrase is found in *Don Quixote*, Part 1, Chapter 21, at the very beginning of the chapter: 'paréceme, Sancho, que no hay refrán que no sea verdadero, porque todos son sentencias sacadas de la misma experiencia, madre de las ciencias todas. . . ' 'I am sure, Sancho, that there is no proverb that is not true, for they are all maxims drawn from the same experience, which is the mother of all knowledge. . . ' In the latter case, especially the final 'concise definition' is the result of considerable transformation in the process of transmission. See *The Home Book of Proverbs: Maxims and Familiar Phrases* (ed. B. Stevenson; New York: Macmillan, 1948), pp. 1905-1906.

actually display the conciseness, insight and sensitivity to sound characteristic of that which they are describing. These definitions are themselves proverbial!

What makes the Hebrew proverbs an apt subject for this study, therefore, is that they are significant and memorable forms of expression precisely because of the way that the words set down the truth. As von Rad says, with regard to Prov. 11.2a (*bā' zādôn wayyābō' qālôn*):

> The assonant form. . . again reminds us what outstanding importance attaches to the word that pins down these garnered truths—only by being formulated is the truth given its sanction.[1]

For example, in the saying 'Birds of a feather flock together', the imagery asserts that similar types of people tend to form groups. And the way the language is used emphasizes that assertion. The alliteration of:

feather flock together
f ther f   ther

is a perfect poetic union of sound and sense—the sounds conveying the meaning actually 'flock together' themselves! And the ellipsis of 'same' before 'feather' helps tighten the unity. It is just these devices, imagery, choice of vocabulary, sound patterning and ellipsis, working together in one line that make this a proverbial utterance. The proverb does not develop its statement on the same scale as a long poem, but it makes effective use of poetic devices nonetheless. The words 'Birds of the same kind congregate in one group' are just not as effective in conveying the truth. Without the use of poetic devices this could just as easily be an excerpt from a scientific journal or from a magazine devoted to natural history.

A study of the sayings of Proverbs will provide an illustration of how literary analysis can be an aid not only for describing the text, but also for understanding it as well. Although the consideration of sound patterns is only one aspect of literary analysis, it inevitably leads to a recognition of many other factors allied with sound patterns that are at work in the proverb. These factors jolt the ear and the

1. G. von Rad, *Old Testament Theology*. I. *The Theology of Israel's Historical Traditions* (trans. D.M.G. Stalker; New York: Harper & Row, 1962), p. 419 and n. 5.

mind, force new insights and challenge set ways of thinking about and customary habits of dealing with the world. It is a way of presenting the familiar in an unfamiliar, thought-provoking fashion. And the starkness or vividness of the language refuses to let the point be obscured. It is a language which amuses, delights and upsets. The argument of this study is basically a demonstration that the biblical proverbs display similar uses of sound, structure and sense, and for the same purpose.

II

So far, the presence of conscious sound patterning in biblical Hebrew poetry has been readily assumed without resort to much supporting argumentation. But questions can arise. First of all, it can be objected that the precise quality of the vowels in the Hebrew text is difficult to determine because OT Hebrew is a dead language. Secondly, OT Hebrew, like other west Semitic languages and Semitic languages in general, has affixing structures (case endings, nominal prefixes, verbal prefixes and suffixes, monographic prepositions, etc.), which form a subset of sounds that necessarily become common in the language. Can their presence in a text be considered conscious sound patterning, especially when the affixing structures account for most of the vocalic or consonantal repetition occurring in the language? And thirdly, should word repetition be treated as conscious sound patterning or simply be regarded as a lexical pattern?[1] If such structures cannot be allowed as part of sound patterns in the language, then all the vowels and half the consonants of OT Hebrew, whether actually functioning as affixes or not, are excluded as legitimate raw material for the type of analysis attempted here. That would just about preclude the very possibility of sound patterns in biblical Hebrew altogether.

The best answer to these problems will be the numerous examples of sound patterns in the Hebrew proverbs to be presented in the following chapters. But in order to demonstrate that this kind of analysis is legitimate, one need only examine the many instances of sound patterning in other languages (particularly dead languages) with affixing structures, such as in biblical Hebrew. One such language is

1. These are problems raised by M. O'Connor, 'The Rhetoric of the Kilamuwa Inscription', *BASOR* 226 (1977), pp. 16-17.

Latin. Fortunately, studies of the Latin poets' use of sound are not in the primitive state in which this aspect of OT poetry finds itself. The examples could easily be multiplied but only their quality is of significance and so just a few will suffice. The examples will deal with first the question of word repetition, then affixes and finally vowels.

The first example, from Virgil (*Aen.* 2.313), has word repetition involving an obvious sound pattern that can hardly be ignored:

exoritur clamorque virum clamorque tubarum.[1]
or ur orque rum orque rum

Two-thirds of this line involve nominal endings with the repetition of suffixed *-que* as well. Another example involving word repetition is from Lucretius (*De rer. nat.* 5.993) and describes primitive man as subject to the attacks of wild beasts:

viva videns vivo sepiliri viscera busto.[2]
v v v v v v

The consonance in /v/ is a clear example of sound patterning. Any phonic analysis that disregards the word repetition, *viva/vivo*, is simply inadequate.

Much closer to the Hebrew are examples provided by Ugaritic literature. The following lines are from the battle scene in the Baal-Mot epic.[3]

1. (20)*mt. ʿz. bʿl. ʿz.* *ʿz ʿz* *ʿl*	(Now) Mot dominates, (now) Baal dominates;
2. *ymṣḫn.* (21) *klsmm.* *mṣ smm* *kl*	They stamp like steeds;

1. 'There arises the clamor of men and the blare of trumpets.' J. Marouzeau, *Traité de stylistique appliquée au latin* (Collection d'études latines, Série scientifique, 12; Paris: Société d'Edition, 1935), p. 52; L.P. Wilkinson, *Golden Latin Artistry* (Cambridge: Cambridge University Press, 1963), p. 56.

2. 'Seeing his body buried alive in a living tomb.' Wilkinson, *Golden Latin Artistry*, p. 52; Marouzeau, *Traité de stylistique*, p. 27.

3. M. Dietrich, O. Loretz and J. Sanmartín, *Die Keilalphabetischen Texte aus Ugarit.* I. *Transkription* (AOAT 24.1; Kevelaer: Verlag Butzon & Bercker; Neukirchen–Vluyn: Neukirchener Verlag, 1976), 1.6.6.20-22.

3. *mt. ql.* (22) *b'l. ql.* (Now) Mot falls, (now) Baal falls.
ql *ql*
'l

4. *'ln. . .* Thereupon. . .
'l

The alliteration of the quickly repeating words (*mt, b'l, 'z*, and *ql*) in these few lines is hardly by chance. Their sounds underscore the ever-reversing fortunes of the combatants: Now Mot, now Baal; one is strong, then the other; one falls, then the other. These sounds are complemented by other sounds: the sibilant and /m/ consonance in the second line and the consonance of /k/ and /q/ plus /l/ that begins in the second line and continues into the third line. Even the first word of the fourth line, *'ln*, echoes the sounds of /'/ and /l/ in both the first and third lines. It is very likely that the rarer word *lsm* was chosen over the normal *ss* for the sake of the pattern.[1] Yet the consonants /m/, /t/, /b/, /'/, /l/, /z/, and /q/ occur in repeating words and most of these, /m/, /t/, /b/, /l/, and /z/, plus /k/, also belong to the subset of commonly used affixes!

To deal more explicitly with the question of affixes, therefore, the following examples will demonstrate their use in sound patterns. In the first, Virgil (*Aen.* 2.210-11) describes the serpents who attack Laocoön in this fashion:[2]

Ardentisque oculos suffecti sanguine et igni
s *s s* *s*
Sibila lambebant linguis vibrantibus ora
s *s* *s*
b l l b b l b b

The consonance in /s/ may or may not be onomatopoeic echoing of the hissing of the serpents; but it is certainly a sound pattern that cannot be ignored. Four of the sibilants involved are parts of nominal affixes. One belongs to a prepositional building element prefixed to a verb. There is still more. The licking tongues of the serpents might possibly be echoed by the /l, b, b/ phonic motif in the second line, a motif which links the very words describing that action. However it is to be

1. B. Margalit, 'Alliteration in Ugaritic Poetry: Its Rôle in Composition and Analysis', *UF* 11 (1979), p. 540.

2. 'With blazing eyes and covered with blood and fire they were licking their hissing mouths with quivering tongues.' Marouzeau, *Traité de stylistique*, p. 28.

evaluated, this sound pattern, too, is clear. A sound pattern built completely on the same verbal suffix comes from Plautus (*Capt.* 134):[1]

Macesco et consenesco et tabesco miser.
esco esco esco

The verb forms are clearly chosen for the sake of the sounds and illustrate phenomena in Hebrew like the use of the *niphal* absol. inf. in the form *hiqqāṭēl* with *yiqqāṭēl*, and in the form *niqṭōl* with *niqṭal*.[2]

Two English examples where the ear of the English speaker is immediately attuned to the issue involved will bring the point home. The /ed/ verbal suffixes and the /s/ patterns are clearly part of the rhyme in the following lines from G.M. Hopkins's poem *God's Grandeur* (vv. 6-7)[3] even though they belong to a common set of affixes in the English language.

And all is seared with trade; bleared, smeared with toil;
eared eared eared
s s s
And wears man's smudge and shares man's smell: the soil. . .
s s s s s s s

A.E. Housman's poem *Reveille* (vv. 9-11) uses an /ing/ end rhyme:

Up, lad, up, 'tis late for lying. . .
ing
Hark, the empty highways crying.
ing

Affixes clearly have a very significant role to play in sound patterning.

As far as the pronunciation of vowels is concerned, biblical Hebrew is not unique in this regard. Analyses of poetry in Elizabethan English, for example, and even more so in ancient Latin poetry face similar problems, which involve the pronunciation of consonants too. But ancient Hebrew morphology is not an area where complete subjectivity reigns and, in fact, there is some vowel notation independent of

1. 'Miserable, I am getting thin, I grow old, I pine away.' Marouzeau, *Traité de stylistique*, p. 111.

2. P. Joüon, *Grammaire de l'hébreu biblique* (Rome: Pontifical Biblical Institute, corr. photo. edn, 1965), §51.b.

3. Unless otherwise noted, all poetic passages are taken from *The Norton Anthology of Poetry* (ed. A.W. Allison *et al.*; New York: W.W. Norton, rev. shorter edn, 1975).

the Masoretic pointing. Can the repeating /l/ of Prov. 15.12 be considered as legitimate raw material for sound patterns, but not the repeating long /o/ vowels of Prov. 15.32?

Prov. 15.12[1] a. *l' y'hb lṣ hwkḥ lw*
l l l
b. *'l ḥkmym l' ylk*
l l l

Prov. 15.32[2] a. *pôrēa' mûsār mô 'ēs napšô*
ô ô ô
b. *wᵉšômēa ' tôkaḥat qôneh lēb*
ô ô ô

A Latin example is the heavy repetition of sounds in this line from Ennius (*Ann.* 109):[3]

O Tite tute Tati tibi tanta tyranne tulisti
t t t t t t t t t t t t
ti ti ti ty ti
ta ta ta
te te
tu tu

Ennius's line is such a *tour de force* that it is hard to imagine that the excessive sound patterns were accidental. Caution is needed, surely. No modern critic is capable of analysing sound patterns involving vowels or consonants in ancient Hebrew with the precision of a David. Modern Latin stylists cannot do that today for Virgil with the sureness of a Quintilian. The only point to be made is that a modern phonic analysis of Hebrew poetry has a claim to legitimacy not unlike a modern phonic analysis of classical Latin poetry.

This raises the question of intentionality: did the Hebrew poets really intend to put sound patterning into their texts? A distinction must be made. The movement 'People United to Save Humanity' chose that title for itself so it could produce the acronym 'PUSH'. There is clearly a conscious, rational process behind the choice of language here. The extent to which the sound patterns in Latin poetry (or Hebrew) are the product of such a conscious plan or the result of a

1. For a fuller discussion, see Chapter 2.
2. For a fuller discussion, see Chapter 6.
3. 'O tyrant Titus Tatius, you brought upon yourself so many things.' Marouzeau, *Traité de stylistique*, p. 44.

more general intention to produce patterned and pleasing speech can never be known. Pleasing sounds in speech can come very naturally, as the girl spoken of before, whose friend Harry could only be described as 'horrible', proves.[1] A literary critic has said that such vowel and consonant patterns 'are seldom consciously worked out by the poet. . . The pattern seems to occur to the poet as a melody may to a composer.'[2] The poet's function may lie more in the area of controlling such effects than producing them. Thus, if alliteration is in a text, it is there and can be studied as such, whether consciously arrived at or not.

III

No overview of the subject that this study presents can hope to reflect fully the rich variety of sound patterns in the individual proverbs. Nor is it possible at this stage to formulate a fully developed theory about sound patterns. Rather, what is needed is further collection and study of examples, or examples that can provide a basis on which a theory can be formulated later on. This study, consequently, will collect and arrange various examples of sound patterns from the proverbs in only a general way, not intending the categories used to be regarded as all-inclusive or permanently fixed. They represent only a beginning in the process of understanding these figures of sound.

With these limits in mind, then, this study of sound patterns will be organized as follows. The next chapter will explain the methodology and terminology to be used (including assonance, consonance and alliteration) and then introduce specific examples illustrating basic forms of sound patterning. Each chapter after this will follow the same general format of an introduction to a particular topic and then a longer section of proverbial texts for analysis that illustrates the topic. Chapter 3 will deal with what will be called 'linking sound patterns', those which join only some of the words in the colon of a particular proverb. Sound patterns which join particular, important words in each colon of a proverb (correlation) will be covered in the next

1. See above, p. 12.

2. D.I. Masson, 'Vowel and Consonant Patterns in Poetry', in *Essays on the Language of Literature* (ed. S. Chatman and S.R. Levin; Boston: Houghton Mifflin, 1967), p. 3.

chapter. Chapter 5 will begin a section on 'tagging sound patterns', those which, by the use of sounds, punctuate and mark off syntactical or semantic units in a proverb. This type of sound pattern will be further explored in Chapter 6 with the 'coordinating' proverb. These proverbs simply juxtapose syntactical units of a proverb (such as the subject and predicate) without conjunction or copula, and the sound patterns often reflect these juxtapositions. Chapter 7 will apply all the techniques examined so far to those proverbs which use word repetition or word play. Such a recurrence of the same or similar words, of course, necessarily involves the repetition of the same or similar sounds and so the study of them is a fitting reprise and conclusion to the whole investigation. Along the way there will be opportunities to show the cogency of sound patterns as an opposing, or even a corroborating, argument for textual changes.

Chapter 2

Basic Sound Patterns

Introduction

Sound patterns created from the simple materials of consonants and vowels help language achieve beauty and expressiveness. An example is found in these lines from A. Pope's poem *Rape of the Lock* (2.131-34):

Or alum styptics with contracting power
i i i i
Shrink his thin essence like a riveled flower:
i i i i
Or, as Ixion fixed, the wretch shall feel
i i
The giddy motion of the whirling mill. . .
i i i

The constant repetition of the /i/ vowel, in both accented and unaccented syllables, gives emphasis and unity to the piece while at the same time providing a tight sound that reflects the general theme of 'contracting' and 'shrinking'.[1] The proverb 'A stitch in time saves nine' is remembered because of the *way* the idea is expressed: the repetition of /s/ in 'stitch' and 'saves' and the rhyme between 'time' and 'nine'. The idea is not new or original, but its mode of expression is striking and attractive.

Sound patterns can determine whether or not certain words amount to a proverb. As seen in the previous chapter, the fact that the brief statement 'Birds of the same kind congregate in one group' has no appealing or catching sound pattern dooms the expression to oblivion. 'Not enough and very tardy' says basically the same thing as 'Too

1. Analysed by C. Brooks and R.P. Warren (eds.), *Understanding Poetry* (New York: Holt, Rinehart and Winston, 4th edn, 1976), p. 524.

little, too late', and almost as concisely, but it is only the latter that is proverbial. The first example lacks the symmetry of carefully arranged sounds and repeating words, which would change it from a limp, prosaic statement into something memorable. The actual proverb works precisely because of its sound patterning: the repetition of the consonant sequence /t, l, t/ in both 'too little' and 'too late', and the initial repetition of the word 'too' in both halves of the saying. The symmetry of sounds distinguishes this type of utterance from everyday speech and creates expressive, memorable and pleasing combinations of words and phrases.

Granted the importance of sound patterning, then, how is it achieved? Noticeable recurrence of the same or similar sounds is the essence of sound patterning in poetry. A contemporary critic states:

> The tissue of most verse forms a web of sound-patterning, often related to sense and mood; the poet may not have worked for it, the reader may not be aware of it, but the words were chosen, and the reader/listener reacts, under its influence; words first chosen may 'attract' others of like sound, which then seem to reinforce their aura.[1]

By sound patterning a mere sequence of words is effectively united; each word is joined to another by the recurrence and attraction of like sounds. Words of different meaning are drawn together by similarities in sound.[2] Such common phrases as 'near and dear', 'part and parcel', and 'forgive and forget' are created by the repetition of consonants and syllables which draw the words together. The effect is strong enough indeed to preserve a phrase even when one member-word has become obsolete: 'might and main', 'kith and kin'. But even words unrelated in meaning can be drawn together by sound. Thus, in the fifth verse of J. Keats's 'Ode on a Grecian Urn', the words 'leaf-fringed legend' become an organic whole through the sound pattern /l, f, f, nged, l, gend/. E.A. Poe's choice of the words 'raven' and 'nevermore' provides his poem *The Raven* with a recurring mirror-image phonic device: /r, v, n/—/n, v, r/.[3] Stanzas 8, 14, 15, 16 and 17

1. Masson, 'Sound in Poetry', p. 785.
2. Casanowicz, *Paronomasia in the Old Testament*, pp. 4-5; Jakobson, 'Closing Statement', p. 371.
3. Jakobson, 'Closing Statement', p. 372. The poem is quoted from *Complete Poems of Edgar Allen Poe* (ed. L. Untermeyer; New York: Hermitage Press, 1943), pp. 101-105.

of the poem all end with the refrain: 'Quoth the Raven, "Nevermore"' (/n, v, r/). In stanza 8 the device also appears in vv. 3 and 4:

> 'Though thy crest be shorn and shaven, thou,' I said, 'art sure no craven,
> r v n
> Ghastly grim and ancient raven wandering from the Nightly shore. . . '
> r v n

Here the other half of the device, /r, v, n/, is repeated in 'craven' and 'raven' and is suggested in the words 'shorn' (/r, n/), 'shaven' (/v, n/), and in the phrase 'sure no' (/r, n/). In the last stanza the full device appears in the first verse rather than the last:

> And the Raven, never flitting, still is sitting, still is sitting. . .
> r v n n v r

In this verse, too, notice the chiasmus, not only of /r, v, n/—/n, v, r/, but also of 'flitting' and 'still' (/litt/—/till/). Only the word 'nevermore' occurs in the last verse of that stanza. The symmetry of sound patterning, therefore, can produce not only pleasure and beauty, but also harmony and unity.

Sound patterns have usually been classified according to what is being repeated. Consonance, as its name implies, is the 'partial or total identity of consonants in words or syllables whose *main* vowels differ'.[1] Thus, 'might and main' has a consonance in /m/, while 'first and last' has a final /st/ sound in each word. In the opening lines of the fourteenth of J. Donne's *Holy Sonnets* there is a consonance combining the labial /b/ (and one /p/) with /r/:

> Batter my heart, three-personed God; for You
> b r r r p r r
> As yet but knock, breathe, shine, and seek to mend;
> b br
> That I may rise and stand, o'erthrow me, and bend
> r r r b
> Your force to break, blow, burn, and make me new.
> r r br b b r

This pattern repeats the sounds of the opening word 'Batter' throughout those lines and complements the forceful imagery of 'battering'. One important point to be noted about consonance is that the main

1. U.K. Goldsmith and S.L. Mooney, 'Consonance', in Preminger (ed.), *Princeton Encyclopedia of Poetry and Poetics*, p. 152.

vowels must differ so as not to create a rhyme like the words 'mend' and 'bend' in the above verses.

The counterpart to this consonance naturally enough deals with the repetition of vowels and is called assonance. It is defined as:

> vowel identity in the tonic syllables, sometimes supported by the same device in the succeeding unstressed syllables, of words whose consonants differ or, if partly the same, avoid creating rhyme[1]. . .

Thus words like 'grave/fate' or 'votive/notice' have vowel identity in /a/ and /o, i/ respectively.[2] In this first stanza of a poem by E. Dickinson, the emphasis on an /ō/ and /ô/ assonance is clear:

The Soul selects her own Society-
ō ō
Then-shuts the Door-
ô
To her divine Majority-
ô
Present no more-
ō ô

More often, however, consonance and assonance go together; that is, similar or identical vowel *and* consonant sounds appear together in words in proximity. This is well illustrated in the tongue-twister 'Peter Piper picked a peck of pickled peppers'. The consonance of /p/, /r/ and /ck/ is immediately apparent as is the assonance in repeating /i/, /ĕ/ and /e/ vowels. This is balanced by other patterns, /p, ĕ, r/, /p, (i, e), ck/ and /pick, ed/ which combine vowel and consonant sounds. A profusion of sound patterning is thus produced:

Peter Piper picked a peck of pickled peppers.
p pp p p p p pp
i i
ĕ ĕ ĕ
e e
r r r
ck ck ck
ed ed

This combination of consonant and vowel identity or similarity in closely related words is usually designated as alliteration:

1. U.K. Goldsmith, 'Assonance', in Preminger (ed.), *Princeton Encyclopedia of Poetry and Poetics*, pp. 53-54.
2. Goldsmith, 'Assonance', p. 54.

> Any repetition of the same sound(s) or syllable in two or more words of a line (or line group), which produces a noticeable artistic effect. . . The most common type of a. is that of initial sounds. . . A. may, however, include with notable effect the repetition of consonants, vowels, or consonant-vowel combinations in medial or even final position. . . [1]

Thus, there is alliteration with the syllable /par/ in 'part and parcel' and the same effect with the sound /forg/ in 'forgive and forget'. With this device whole syllables or combinations of vowels and consonants form the sound pattern joining words.

The three basic classifications, then, are: consonance or consonant repetition, assonance or vowel identity, and alliteration, which combines consonance with assonance to form repeating groups of sounds and syllables. These definitions, however, while precise enough for the purposes of this study, are not universal. Often the term 'alliteration' is used to describe only a pattern of consonant repetition or is restricted even further to apply only to the repetition of initial sounds in words, its original application.[2] But there is no need to explore these distinctions here; the terms will be used according to the definitions already given.

Aside from these three basic classifications of consonance, assonance and alliteration, poetic figures of sound can also be classified according to their various configurations in a line of verse, that is, the patterns created by the many ways in which consonants, vowels or both together can repeat. Obviously attempts to organize the sounds in a line of poetry have their limits. But a certain amount of classification is useful for organizing the discussion because it helps obviate the patterns that otherwise are only vaguely perceived and which might be treated as coincidental or uncontrollable. It must be remembered, too, that these classifications are almost never found in a pure state and nearly always overlap.

These are some of the very basic configurations. A recurrent combination of sounds, whether vowels, consonants or both, is called a

1. U.K. Goldsmith, 'Alliteration', in Preminger (ed.), *Princeton Encyclopedia of Poetry and Poetics*, p. 15.

2. X.J. Kennedy, *An Introduction to Poetry* (New York: Little, Brown & Co., 1966), pp. 125-28; L. Perrine, *Sound and Sense* (New York: Harcourt, Brace, Jovanovich, 4th edn, 1973), pp. 168-69; R.A. Lanham, *A Handlist of Rhetorical Terms* (Berkeley: University of California Press, 1968), p. 6.

motif.[1] So /par/ is a once repeated motif in the phrase 'part and parcel'. A series is a motif in which only one element (consonant or vowel) or only one class of elements (for example, sibilants) is involved. In the following lines from R. Frost's poem *Birches* there are two such series. A series in /s/ opens the lines, is followed by another in /(sh, ch)/ and then returns again to /s/, concluding with a final /st/ sound:

> Soon the sun's warmth makes them shed crystal shells
> s s s s sh s sh s
> Shattering and avalanching on the snowcrust. . .
> sh ch s st

A motif of two or more sounds repeated without a change of order in its elements is called a sequence.[2] The opening words of J. Donne's poem, *A Lecture upon the Shadow*,[3] begins with a sequence in /st, and/:

> Stand still, and I will read to thee. . .
> stand st and

R. Lowell's opening line in *The Public Garden* begins with a full syllable in sequence:

> Burnished, burned-out, still burning as the year. . .
> burn burn burn

If the sounds of the sequence are spaced further apart in the second member, then it is a loosening sequence. The opposite situation is a tightening sequence.[4] Examples of each are found, again, in Lowell's poem, *The Public Garden*. The first is a loosening sequence in /c, r/ which appears at the beginning of the poem:

> The city and its cruising cars surround. . .
> cr c r

Next, a tightening sequence occurs in the second to last line using the sounds /f, l/:

1. D.I. Masson, 'Thematic Analysis of Sounds in Poetry', in Chatman and Levin (eds.), *Essays on the Language of Literature*, p. 55.
2. Masson, 'Vowel Patterns', p. 4.
3. Quoted in Brooks and Warren (eds.), *Understanding Poetry*, p. 243.
4. Masson, 'Vowel Patterns', p. 4.

The fountain's failing waters flash around. . .
f l fl

Finally, there is the chiastic sequence in which the order of the elements is exactly reversed.[1] The third and fourth lines of *Kubla Khan* by S.T. Coleridge have an example using the sequence /r, v/:

Where Alph, the sacred river, ran
r v
Through caverns measureless to man. . .
v r

A final, practical note. When different elements of the same class of consonants appear in one sequence, all those elements are placed in parentheses within the slash marks indicating the sequence. For example, in the following half-line from J. Keats's *Ode to a Nightingale* (7.10),

Charmed magic casements
ch m m g

this chiastic sequence would be written /(ch, g), m/.[2]

The general heading for these sound patterns, consequently, is the motif. If there is only one repeating sound then the first subdivision is the series. Otherwise, the pattern is a sequence, the second subdivision. Then, depending on how the configuration of the sounds in the second member of the sequence relates to the first, the sequence is either tightening, loosening or chiastic. Those sound patterns which seem more random and irregular are called progressions.[3] These categories will be applied to the sound patterns of the Hebrew proverbs, not as definitive, watertight classifications, but as useful guides for starting and directing the analysis. Furthermore, there is no presumption made that these categories or any others, for that matter, are exhaustive or meet all the requirements for a full study of the sounds of Hebrew poetry. Rather, they are meant to suggest types of analysis which could contribute to further, in-depth studies of sound patterns in Hebrew poetry.

1. Masson, 'Vowel Patterns', p. 4.
2. Masson, 'Vowel Patterns', p. 5.
3. Masson, 'Thematic Analysis', p. 56.

Texts

Proverbs 10.12. The first example from the proverbs uses assonance and consonance to create different sound patterns.

a.	*śin'â t*^{e}*'ôrēr m*^{e}*dānîm*	Hatred stirs up disputes,
b.	*w*^{e}*'al kol p*^{e}*šā'îm t*^{e}*kasseh 'ah*^{a}*bâ*	but love covers all offenses.

One pattern is a chiasmus created by the first word *śin'â* sharing a rhyme in final /â/ with its opposite, the last word, *'ah*^{a}*bâ*; *m*^{e}*dānîm* and *p*^{e}*šā'îm* have an /ĕ, ā, îm/ assonance.

a.	*śin'â . . . m*^{e}*dānîm*	b.	*. . . p*^{e}*šā'îm . . . 'ah*^{a}*bâ*
	â ^{e} *ā îm*		^{e} *ā îm* *â*

This pattern actually outlines the basic structure of the proverb, for it is so constructed that, except for the addition of the prepositional phrase *'al kol*, the second colon is a chiastic reflection of the first, semantically and grammatically.

a.	*śin'â*	*t*^{e}*'ôrēr*	*m*^{e}*dānîm*
	subj.	v.	obj.
	A	B	C
b.	*w*^{e}*'al kol p*^{e}*šā'îm*	*t*^{e}*kasseh*	*'ah*^{a}*bâ*
	prep. phrase (obj.)	v.	subj.
	C′	B′	A′

A dramatic tension is thereby created: in the first colon hatred causes disputes to arise, but in the second colon offenses are prevented from escalating into disputes by love. Hatred agitates, love keeps peace.[1]

The first colon contains another phonic motif, a sequence /n, (t, d)/.

a.	*śn'h t'wrr mdnym*
	n t dn

The motif is obviously chiastic and of the tightening type in that the two sounds, found first in two words, the subject and verb, are echoed together in the last word, the object. One last pattern is a sequence in the second colon involving labials and sibilants with /k/: /k, (p, b), (š, s)/.

1. For a different analysis of this text, see M. Dahood, 'Una coppia di termini ugaritici e Prov. 10, 12', *BeO* 15 (1973), pp. 253-54.

b. *w'l kl pš'ym tksh 'hbh*
k pš ks b

It is partially chiastic, too, since the last two elements of the sequence (labials and sibilants) reverse positions in the second member. Both as a whole and in each of its cola, sound patterns tie this proverb quite closely together.

Proverbs 18.13. In this proverb consonance creates a chiastic sound pattern in the first colon.

a. *mēšîb dābār b^e^ṭerem yišmā'*	The one who returns an answer before he listens—
b. *'iwwelet hî' lô ûk^e^limmâ*	his is the folly and the shame.

The chiasmus is formed from two different sequences of sound. The first is formed from the motif /m, š / found in both *mšyb* and *yšm'*; the second sequence uses the motif /(d, ṭ), b, r/ containing the sounds of the words *dābār* and *b^e^ṭerem*. The chiastic sound patterning thus brings the two end words and the two middle words of the first half of the saying together.

a. *mšyb dbr bṭrm yšm'*
mš dbr bṭr šm

The first sequence, /m, š /, is also chiastic in itself, the first member being /mš /, the second /šm/. The first two sounds of the second sequence are also chiastically arranged: /d, b, r/ and /b, ṭ, r/. In addition, a consonance in /b/[1] joins the first three words of the same colon, one in /m/ joins the first word with the last two; and a chiastic sequence /m, b/ joins the first and third word.

a. *mšyb dbr bṭrm yšm'*
m b b b m m

1. The problem of the same consonant having variant non-alliterative pronunciations and the problem of the *begadkephath* letters in particular are ignored here. That introduces a margin of error which is accepted. Otherwise the present study is impossible. It is simply presumed that, for instance, all sounds written *b* were close enough to alliterate. The where and when of the aspiration of the *begadkephath* letters cannot be determined precisely—nor even whether the rules were always the same (see LXX *Thamar, Chanaan, Akchō, Sepphōra*). See the remarks of H.Y. Priebatsch, 'Spiranten und Aspiratae in Ugarit, AT und Hellas', *UF* 12 (1980), pp. 317-33.

The second colon, by contrast, has less sound patterning with just a series in /l/.

b. *'wlt hy' lw wklmh*
l l l

The sound patterns are concentrated in the first colon where the fool is described.

Proverbs 13.7. This proverb has a distinctive quality. Among those proverbs which detail various phenomena by placing simple nominal sentences next to each other in parallel cola (e.g. 10.17; 11.13; 13.3), this saying is one in which phenomena are so organized as to become paradoxical: seeming wealth and great poverty, seeming poverty but great wealth.[1]

a. *yēš mit'aššēr wᵉ'ên kōl*	There's the one who feigns wealth but has nothing,
b. *mitrôšēš wᵉhôn rāb*	and another who feigns poverty but has great wealth.

The different personalities and thus the two cola are obviously related by sound. The introductory word *yēš* relates to both cola by reason of the repetition of the /ēš/ motif in both participles.[2] The participial prefix /mit/ plus /r/ is also repeated in both words. And a chiasmus is created between the two participles by a /r, š / motif.

a. *yēš mit'aššēr . . .*	b. *mitrôšēš . . .*
ēš mit ššēr	*mitr šēš*
šš r	*r š š*

The opposition of meaning in the two participles (poor/rich) is reflected thereby in the reversal of order between those consonants (the chiasmus).

The second half of each colon has the phonic sequence /wĕ, n/ to relate *wᵉ'ên kōl* and *wᵉhôn rāb*, plus the morphological feature that all the words in the second half of each colon are monosyllabic. Within the second colon the /rô/ of *mitrôšēš* is echoed in the /ô/ of *wᵉhôn* and the /r/ of *rāb*, thus creating a chiastic sequence in the colon.

1. Hermisson, *Studien*, pp. 146-48.
2. Boström, *Paronomasi*, p. 140.

a.	. . . *w*^{e}*'ên kōl*	b.	*mitrôšēš w*^{e}*hôn rāb*
	w^{e} *n*		*w*^{e} *n*
			rô *ô r*

The sound patterning rather clearly marks the first and second halves of each colon with similar sounds and relates contrasting things: 'feigning wealth' with 'feigning poverty' and 'having nothing' with 'having plenty'.

Proverbs 16.3. The last word in each colon provides the dominant sound pattern to link the cola of this proverb.

a.	*gōl*[1] *'el* YHWH *ma'*^{a}*śêkā*	Entrust your works to the Lord
b.	*w*^{e}*yikkōnû maḥš*^{e}*bōtêkā*	and your plans will succeed.

The pattern is the sound sequence of /ma, (ś, š), êkā/ with which each colon concludes.[2]

a.	. . . *ma'*^{a}*śêkā*	b.	*maḥš*^{e}*bōtêkā*
	ma śêkā		*ma š êkā*

The second person singular suffix attached to each, prominent already because of its final position in each colon, is further highlighted by the repetition of /k/ in the verb *yikkōnû*. A subpattern of sound is found in the repetition of /ō/ in *yikkōnû* and *maḥš*^{e}*bōtêkā*, which sound first occurs in the imperative *gōl*.

a.	*gōl 'el* YHWH *ma'*^{a}*śêkā*	b.	*w*^{e}*yikkōnû maḥš*^{e}*bōtêkā*
	ō		*ō ō*
	k		*kk k*

Nearly all the words of the proverb are linked by sound.

Proverbs 12.8. The consonant /l/ plays a prominent role in this saying and particularly in the words related by the theme.

a.	*l*^{e}*pî śiklô y*^{e}*hullal 'îš*	According to his good sense is a man praised,
b.	*w*^{e}*na'*^{a}*wēh lēb yihyeh lābûz*	but a twisted mind is to be despised.

The consonant /l/ appears in *śiklô*, 'his good sense', and in its effect,

1. The word *gōl* is *qal* imper. from *gll*, 'roll'. It also seems to have the meaning 'entrust' ('roll towards' ?) as in Pss. 37.5 and 22.9. Otherwise read *gal* with *BHS*.
2. Boström, *Paronomasi*, p. 160.

y^e^hullal, 'he is praised'; then also in a 'twisted *lēb*' and its effect, *lābûz*, 'be despised'. These last two words and their cause and effect relationship share an even stronger link with their /l, b/ sequence,[1] which echoes the /l, p/ pattern in the opening word *l^e^pî*. The verbs are also related because of their shared, initial /y, h/ sequence.[2] This gives the following configuration in the proverb:

a.	*lpy śklw yhll 'yš*	b.	*wn'wh lb yhyh lbwz*
	lp l yhll		*lb yh lb*

The first colon has an additional pattern when the sibilants are included with /l/.

a.	*lpy śklw yhll 'yš*
	l ś l ll š

Thus, the /l, ś, l/ sequence of the first phrase of this colon is repeated in the following verb and its subject. Consequently, hardly any word is left untouched by some sound pattern.[3]

Proverbs 20.18. It is the first two words of each colon particularly that contain the dominant sounds of this proverb.

a.	*maḥ^a^šābôt b^e^'ēṣâ tikkôn*	Plans made with advice succeed,
b.	*ûb^e^taḥbūlôt '^a^śēh milḥāmâ*	so with counsel make war.

The first two words not only share a rhyme in /ôt/, but they also share a consonantal sequence /ḥ, b, t/. The verb *tikkôn* picks up the /t/ of this pattern. In addition, *b^e^'ēṣâ* and *'^a^śēh* share a /', (ṣ, ś)/ sequence.

a.	*mḥšbôt b'ṣh tkwn*	b.	*wbtḥblôt 'śh mlḥmh*
	ḥ bôt 'ṣ t		*btḥb ôt 'ś*

Finally, there is just enough consonance throughout to give each colon an individual sound pattern. The first colon has a repeated sequence

1. Boström, *Paronomasi*, p. 134.
2. Boström, *Paronomasi*, p. 134.
3. At the beginning of the second colon *BHS* suggests *n'bh lb* on the basis of LXX νωθροκάρδιος. That would certainly be favored by the sound pattern of the colon, but OT *'bh* has no attested *niphal* form. The *niphal* form does appear in post-biblical Hebrew; see M. Jastrow, *A Dictionary of the Targumim, the Talmud Babli and Yerushalmi, and the Midrashic Literature* (2 vols.; New York: The Judaica Press, 1975), p. 1037a.

/(š, s), b, t/; the second colon has a chiastic pattern involving the motif /ḥ, l/.

a. *mḥšbwt b'ṣh tkwn* — b. *wbtḥblwt 'śh mlḥmh*
šb t b ṣ t — *ḥ l lḥ*

The tie made between the first word of each colon by consonance and rhyme suggests that synonymous sense was not the only factor that brought these words together in the proverb. The noun *taḥbūlôt* is not a common word, occurring only six times in the OT. It is used once more in conjunction with *maḥšᵉbôt* in Prov. 12.5, where it contributes to the sound patterning of that proverb as well.[1]

Proverbs 20.28. Questions have been raised as to whether the repetition of the word *ḥsd* in this proverb is correct.

a.	*ḥesed we'ᵉmet yiṣṣᵉrû melek*	Mercy and fidelity safeguard a king,
b.	*wᵉsā'ad baḥesed kisᵉ'ô*	and he supports his throne by mercy.

The word repetition involves the word *ḥesed* in both the first and second cola. The thought progression of the saying—from what supports the king to what supports his government—would seem to require a different word in the second colon, such as *ṣedeq* (which is usually suggested).[2] The double use of the word *ḥesed* seems (at least to modern ears) redundant and inelegant. Can sound patterns provide any help?

There are definite sound patterns in the proverb, repeated from colon to colon. The main pattern involves the motif /s, d/ repeated

1. For a full discussion, see Chapter 6.

2. Toy, *A Critical Commentary*, pp. 395-96; B. Gemser, *Sprüche Salomos* (HAT, 16; Tübingen: Mohr [Paul Siebeck], 2nd edn, 1963), p. 79. On the other hand, W.A. van der Weiden (*Le livre des Proverbes: Notes philologiques* [BibOr, 23; Rome: Biblical Institute Press, 1970], pp. 132-33) defends the repetition of *ḥesed* with the suggestion that *ḥesed we'ᵉmet* in v. 28a represents God's gifts to the king and the *ḥesed* in v. 28b is the king's response to the divine generosity. The two words are used in this sense in Ps. 40.12b,

ḥsdk w'mtk tmyd yṣrwny,

and in Ps. 61.8, where the reference is specifically to the king (v. 6),

yšb 'wlm lpny 'lhym
ḥsd w'mt mn ynṣrhw.

twice at the beginning of the second colon. These sounds are echoed by a /t, ṣ/ sequence in the latter half of the first colon, and by the /s/ of *ks'w* in the second colon.

a.	*ḥsd w'mt yṣrw mlk*	b.	*ws'd bḥsd ks'w*
	sd t ṣ		*s d sd s*

If the second *ḥesed* were changed to *ṣedeq*, the second colon sound pattern would be

b.	*ws'd bṣdq ks'w*
	s d ṣd s

a not very noticeable difference. The /q/ of *ṣedeq* would also provide a link with the next word *kis^{e}'ô*. But on the level of sound alone there is no decisive gain from the choice of *ṣedeq* over *ḥesed*.

Proverbs 21.21. This saying is unusual in that the thought of the first colon is continued and completed by the second colon. The majority of the proverbs have separate, though related thoughts in each colon. As in the previous proverb the word *ḥsd* plays a prominent role in the sound patterning.

a.	*rōdēp ṣ^{e}dāqâ wāḥāsed*	Whoever pursues justice and mercy
b.	*yimṣā' ḥayyîm ṣ^{e}dāqā w^{e}kābôd*	will find life, justice, and honor.

The proverb creates a pattern of consonance throughout, using the sequence /(ṣ, s), d/ as the prominent motif.

a.	*rdp ṣdqh wḥsd*	b.	*ymṣ' ḥyym ṣdqh wkbwd*
	d ṣd sd		*ṣ ṣd d*

Three words especially, *ṣ^{e}dāqâ*, *ḥāsed* and the second *ṣ^{e}dāqâ*, make the major contribution to this sound pattern. The only word which does not fit in the sound pattern is *ḥayyîm* in the second colon. This is interesting because there are those who would eliminate a word in the second colon. However, it is not *ḥayyîm*, but rather the second *ṣ^{e}dāqâ*. Toy comments about this repeated word: 'to say that he who follows righteousness finds righteousness is meaningless'.[1] This stance is supported by metrical analysis. The second *ṣ^{e}dāqâ* gives the proverb

1. Toy, *A Critical Commentary*, pp. 406-407; R.B.Y. Scott (*Proverbs. Ecclesiastes* [AB, 18; Garden City, NY: Doubleday, 1965], p. 124 n. f) also deletes the word without comment.

an unbalanced 3:4 meter, a lack of balance also visible in terms of the syllable count (8:10) and the grammatical parallelism:

a. part. + obj. + obj. (= subj.)
b. verb + obj. + obj. + obj. (= pred.)

Finally, the LXX eliminates the word altogether and this fact would seem to clinch the argument.[1]

However, in terms of sound patterning, there is something that can be said for the present MT version of the proverb. An alliterative sequence /yim, ṣ/, which occurs in the first word of the second colon, the verb *yimṣā'*, is repeated in the very next phrase, and suggests that both *ḥyym* and *ṣdqh* belong to the colon.[2]

b. *yimṣā' ḥayyîm ṣ^e^dāqâ wkbwd*
yimṣ *yîm ṣ*

The syllable /ḥa/ of *ḥayyîm*, furthermore, taken together with the /ṣĕd/ of *ṣ^e^dāqâ*, seems to echo the *ḥāsed* of the previous colon.

a. *rpd ṣdqh wāḥāsed* b. *ymṣ' ḥayyîm ṣ^e^dāqâ wkbwd*
ḥāsed *ḥa* *ṣ^e^d*

Such echoing sounds would not be improbable in a saying that already utilizes such devices: namely, the recurrence of the /ōd/ from *rōdēp* at the end of the saying in *kābôd*, the chiasmus of the /d, (b, p)/ motif in the same two words, and the /ṣ, ḥ/ of *ṣdqh wḥsd* in the first colon repeated in *ymṣ' ḥyym* in the second. In terms of sound, consequently, neither *ḥyym* nor *ṣdqh* need be regarded as a plus.

It is true that the major dental and sibilant consonance of the proverb has been broken by *ḥyym*. But that break could merely be indicating that a conclusion to the first statement will not only re-echo the first statement but will even add more. That is, the one who pursues *ṣdqh* will also receive *ṣdqh* and more besides: *ḥyym* and *kbwd*! The 3:4 imbalance could be intended to suggest this—the reward for practising *ṣdqh* is even more abundant than *ṣdqh* itself! The fact that the present MT gives evidence of cohesive sound

1. Gemser (*Sprüche*, p. 81), H. Ringgren and W. Zimmerli (*Sprüche. Prediger* [ATD, 16.1; Göttingen: Vandenhoeck & Ruprecht, 1962], p. 84), and W. McKane (*Proverbs: A New Approach* [London: SCM Press, 1970], pp. 556-57) all cite the LXX deletion when eliminating the word themselves.
2. Boström, *Paronomasi*, p. 186.

patterning, and can have a reasonable interpretation besides, cautions against hasty judgments, preferring either the LXX or the MT. One text need not necessarily be a 'mistake'; both can be valid, justifiable versions, each on its own terms.

Proverbs 13.6. Rhyme joins the first words of each colon in a clear phonic link.

a.	*ṣ^{e}dāqâ tiṣṣōr tom dārek*	Virtue protects the one who walks honestly,
b.	*w^{e}riš'â t^{e}sallēp ḥaṭṭā't*	but wickedness overturns the sinner.

The rhyme in /â/ between *ṣ^{e}dāqâ* and *riš'â* joins semantically antithetic terms which have the same syntax as subjects in their respective cola. In addition, a chiastic repetition of the sequence /ṣ, (d, t)/ occurs in the first colon and is picked up again by a /t, s/ sequence in the verb *tslp* in the second colon. Dentals (ṭ, t, d) tie *tm drk* from the first colon to *ḥṭ't*, the last word of the saying.

a.	*ṣ^{e}dāqâ tiṣṣōr*	*tom dārek*
	ṣ d â t ṣṣ	*t d*
b.	*w^{e}riš'â t^{e}sallēp*	*ḥaṭṭā't*
	š â t s	*ṭṭ t*

The sound patterns generally follow the grammatical and semantic parallelism of the saying:

	subj	+	v.	+	obj.
a.	*ṣ^{e}dāqâ*		*tiṣṣōr*		*tom dārek*
	A		B		C
b.	*w^{e}riš'â*		*t^{e}sallēp*		*ḥaṭṭā't*
	A′		B′		C′

There are other interpretations of how the proverb should be understood. The number of abstract nouns in the saying is a problem. The solutions offered generally concern the second colon. One takes *ḥaṭṭā't* as subject in that colon and treats *riš'â* as an abstract noun used for a concrete collective.[1] This is quite possible and only changes the parallelism between the cola into a chiastic arrangement. But the rhyme and antithetic parallelism between *ṣdqh* and *rš'h* would be at odds with the grammatical use of those words—the former is a subject, the latter an object. Furthermore, if *rš'h* were changed to

1. Gemser, *Sprüche*, p. 112; Ringgren, *Sprüche*, p. 55.

r^{e}šā'îm,[1] not only would the grammatical parallelism be gone, but the rhyme in /â/ as well. Another emendation reads *ḥaṭṭā'îm* instead of *ḥaṭṭā't*.[2] This would also be possible but requires a change in the text and would decrease the dental euphony between the cola. Besides, the use of *ḥaṭṭā't* as an abstract noun for a concrete individual is quite possible.[3] Whichever interpretation is followed, the proverb illustrates how important sound patterns can be. No poetic text should be emended without considering how the sounds of the verse will be affected.

Proverbs 12.25. In this proverb sound patterns take precedence over rules of grammar.

a.	*d^{e}'āgâ b^{e}leb 'îš yašḥennâ*	Anxiety in a man's heart depresses it,
b.	*w^{e}dābār ṭôb y^{e}śamm^{e}ḥennâ*	but a kind word makes it happy.

From the point of view of consonance and assonance this proverb works very well. The subject phrase in each colon, *d^{e}'āgâ b^{e}leb* and *w^{e}dābār ṭôb*, has the same sequence /d, b, b/:

a. *d'gh blb 'yš yšḥnh*
d b b

b. *wdbr ṭwb yśmḥnh*
db b

1. *BHK*; also A. Barucq, *Le livre des Proverbs* (SB; Paris: Gabalda, 1964), p. 120.
2. Toy, *A Critical Commentary*, p. 266.
3. Abstract nouns used for the concrete are a fairly common device in Hebrew. It is treated in F.E. König, *Historisch-kritisches Lehrgebäude der hebräischen Sprache*. II.2. *Historisch-comparative Syntax der hebräischen Sprache* (Leipzig: Hinrichs, 1897), §243.a. This topic is taken up again in M. Dahood, *Psalms*. III. *Psalms 101–150* (AB; New York: Doubleday, 1965–1970), pp. 411-12. This particular proverb was used as an example of this very device by W.A. van der Weiden, '"Abstractum pro concreto", phaenomenon stilisticum', *VD* 44 (1966), p. 51. F. Zorell, *Lexicon hebraicum et aramaicum Veteris Testamenti* (Rome: Pontificium Institutum Biblicum, 1954), p. 234a, suggests reading *ḥaṭṭa't* in Prov. 13.6b as 'sinner' (*peccator*) by metonymy. He also holds out the possibility that the word is a *nomen agentis* (*qaṭṭal + t*), though masculine, as in *qōhelet* (p. 234b). Metonymy could also explain the Masoretic pointing of *tom* in the first colon, although, oddly enough, Zorell prefers to read *tam* there (p. 900b) with *BHK* and *BHS*.

And both predicates have their own identical pattern:

a. . . .*yašḥennâ* b. . . . *y^e^śamm^e^ḥennâ*
y šḥennâ *y ś ḥennâ*

Finally, the first and last words of the first colon and the last word of the proverb share the same end rhyme:[1]

a. *d^e'āgâ blb 'yš yašḥennâ* b. *wdbr ṭwb y^e^śamm^e^ḥennâ*
â ḥennâ *ḥennâ*

The sound patterns clearly align and relate the contrasting pairs of words.

But as an example of good grammar the proverb fails. If the gender agreement between *leb* and the verbal suffix is correct, then this is the only time *leb* is feminine. Clear grammatical disagreement also occurs between the feminine subject *d^e^'āgâ* and its verb *yašḥennâ* with its masculine prefix /y/.[2] This form of the verb with its /y/ prefix can readily be explained as an accommodation to the verb in the second colon (*y^e^śamm^e^ḥennâ*) for the sake of euphony. The same consideration can be applied to the feminine verbal suffixes with their reference back to either *'îš* or *leb*, each of which is masculine. Here again correct grammar has been affected by euphony. The two suffixes have been accommodated to create an end rhyme in /a/ with the opening word *d^e^'āgâ*. It is also possible that the *-ennâ* forms are to be understood as remnants of the old energic, and the object of the verbs (*'îš* or *leb*) is simply understood. In any case to change the *-ennâ* forms to *-enhū* or *-ennû*[3] would eliminate some of the sound patterning.

The use of such energic forms for the sake of sound is not without parallel. In Prov. 1.20 the energic form *tārōnnâ* at the end of the first colon is used to create rhyme with *qôlāh*, the last word in the line.[4] It

1. Boström, *Paronomasi*, p. 138.

2. BDB, p. 524, lists Prov. 12.25 as the only instance of *leb* as feminine. The grammatical disagreement between subject and verb is eased by the tendency of the Masoretes to replace the feminine verbal form by the masculine; see Joüon, *Grammaire*, §150.k.

3. *BHS*; McKane (*Proverbs*, pp. 229 and 446) reads 'him', as does Scott, (*Proverbs*, p. 90).

4. Toy, *A Critical Commentary*, p. 30. Toy was working before such energic forms, apart from situations where the energic appears on the end of the imperfect before suffixes, were attested as a regular feature of any west Semitic language. At

is also worth noting how at the beginning of the same verse the plural *ḥokmôt* is used with a singular verb to fit the /o/ assonance throughout the line, but especially to rhyme with *bārᵉḥōbôt* at the beginning of the second colon.

This takes care of the problem with the verbal suffixes, but still leaves the one concerning the gender agreement between *dᵉ'āgâ* and its verb. Changing the verb to *tšḥnh* in order to agree with *dᵉ'āgâ*, however, erases the initial consonance between the two verbs. Even such a small change, therefore, begins to unravel the clear sound patterning. The better solution to the whole gender disagreement question seems to be the simple assumption that the forms were chosen regardless of the grammar for the sake of sound.

Proverbs 19.5. This proverb illustrates how one colon can be reflected mirror-like in the second colon, with the sound binding the two parts of the saying together.

a.	*'ēd šᵉqārîm lō' yinnāqeh*	A false witness will not go unpunished,
b.	*wᵉyāpîaḥ kᵉzābîm lō' yimmālēṭ*	and a lying witness will not escape.

Each colon has an identical and elaborate sound sequence after the initial word:[1]

a.	. . . *šᵉqārîm lō' yinnāqeh*	b.	. . . *kᵉzābîm lō' yimmālēṭ*
	ᵉ ā îm lō' yi ā e		*ᵉ ā îm lō' yi ā ē*

The entire phonic sequence includes the masculine plural noun form followed by the negative particle and ends with the *niph'al* form of the verb. The *yqṭl* verb forms (*ynqh* and *ymlṭ*) also form a bond. These patterns clearly emphasize the parallelism by their exact duplication of sounds in each colon. The saying, in effect, displays double parallelism—sound and sense. The vowel patterns add their own chiastic structure: the sequence of /ā/ and /i/ vowels is reversed after the *lō'* in each colon.

Each colon differs from the other only in its first word: *'ēd* for the first colon and *wᵉyāpîaḥ* for the second, although it should be noted

that time the skepticism about such forms, registered in GKC, §47.k, was justified. However, Ugaritic has changed the situation. For a critical evaluation of the *status quaestionis* in Hebrew, see D.A. Robertson, *Linguistic Evidence in Dating Early Hebrew Poetry* (SBLDS, 3; Missoula, MT: Scholars Press, 1972), pp. 112-18.

1. Boström, *Paronomasi*, p. 175.

that the vowel sequence in *w^e^yāpîaḥ* duplicates the /ā, î/ vowel sequence in the next word, *k^e^zābîm*. The *'ēd*, on the other hand, has a weak phonic counterpart with the last syllable (*-ēṭ*) of the last word, *yimmālēṭ*, forming thereby a kind of phonic 'inclusion'.[1] The word *yāpîaḥ*, a substantive paralleling *'ēd* of the first colon and in a genitive relationship with *k^e^zābîm*, is the subject of *yimmālēṭ*, and a perfect complement to the prefix tense sequence of *yinnāqeh. . . yimmālēṭ*, with just the reversal of the vowel sequence from /i, a/ to /a, i/.[2]

Proverbs 19.9. This variant form of the preceding proverb differs from it by only one word and provides an interesting contrast.

a. *'ēd š^e^qārîm lō' yinnāqeh*	A false witness will not go unpunished,
b. *w^e^yāpîaḥ k^e^zābîm yō'bēd*	and a lying witness *will perish*.

The description of sound patterning in Prov. 19.5 will suffice for Prov. 19.9 with a few changes. For example, the second colon of 19.9 has a different sequence of sounds, /y, (p, b)/, and repeats the /b/ in *kzbym*:

b. *wypyḥ kzbym y'bd*
yp b y b

Although the assonance with the verb *yinnāqeh* is gone, the new word, *yō'bēd*, resumes the /ō/ vowel of *lō'* from the first colon and parallels more clearly than *yimmālēṭ* the /ēd/ sound of *'ēd* from the beginning of the proverb. A chiastic formation is thus created, involving the phrases *'ēd š^e^qārîm lō'* and *k^e^zābîm yō'bēd*:

a.	*'ēd š^e^qārîm lō'* . . .	b.	. . . *k^e^zābîm yō'bēd*
	ēd îm ō		*îm ō ēd*

This version of the proverb, therefore, uses *yō'bēd* to strengthen the link between beginning and end, a link less prominently reflected in the *'ēd–yimmālēṭ* pattern of 19.5.

Proverbs 27.14. The most obvious literary characteristic of this proverb is oxymoron whereby the blessing (*mbrk*) becomes a curse (*qllh*).

1. Boström, *Paronomasi*, p. 175.
2. On *ypyḥ* see D. Pardee, '*YPḤ* "Witness" in Hebrew and Ugaritic', *VT* 28 (1978), pp. 204-13; P.D. Miller, '*YĀPÎAḤ* in Psalm xii 6', *VT* 29 (1979), pp. 495-501.

a. *m^e bārēk rē'ēhû b^e qôl gādôl babbōqer haškêm*	Whoever greets his neighbor with a loud voice early in the morning
b. *q^e lālâ tēḥāšeb lô*	should be regarded as a curse.

Because the proverb appears to be too long[1] various emendations have been suggested. Gemser deletes the phrase *babbōqer haškêm* 'metri causa'.[2] Toy says the same phrase is 'unnecessary, mars the rhythmical symmetry, and is properly to be omitted as a gloss'.[3] On the other hand Delitzsch has proposed that the very length of the first colon could be intended to illustrate the heavy and pretentious greeting being given, the reason why the greeting goes from blessing to curse.[4] The first colon with fifteen syllables is twice as long as the second with its seven syllables. Scott has suggested that *bbqr hškym* is simply a variant for *bqwl gdwl*.[5] Can an analysis of the sound patterns shed any light on these problems?

In the first colon the most obvious sounds are those of /b/, /r/ and /k, q, g/:

```
a.  mbrk r'hw bqwl gdwl bbqr hškym
     b         b         bb
      r r                  r
       k        q  g       q    k
```

These sounds provide a constant echo of the first word *mbrk*. The second colon repeats /q/ from the first and then concludes with a series in /l/:

```
b.  qllh tḥšb lw
    qll       l
```

There are other sound patterns. The first words of each phrase in the first colon follow the sequence /b, (k, q)/:

1. Boström (*Paronomasi*, p. 81) thinks v. 14a is too full with some words susceptible of a later dating. As an example he suggests that *haškêm* is unnecessary.

2. Gemser, *Sprüche*, p. 97.

3. Toy, *A Critical Commentary*, p. 488. The *BHS* notes that one Hebrew MS deletes the phrase.

4. F. Delitzsch, *Commentary on the Old Testament*. VI.2. *Biblical Commentary on the Proverbs of Solomon* (6 vols.; trans. J. Martin and M.G. Easton; Grand Rapids, MI: Eerdmans, 1976), p. 209.

5. Scott, *Proverbs*, p. 163.

a. *mbrk r'hw bqwl gdwl bbqr hškym*
b k bq bbq

The first two phrases, furthermore, have their own sound patterns. An alliteration in /rē/ links *m*^{e}*bārēk rē'ēhû*, while the sound of /ôl/ binds *b*^{e}*qôl gādôl* together. The latter phrase has an echo in the second colon based on the sequence /(q, g), l/ and again the sound of /ôl/.

a. . . .*b*^{e}*qôl gādôl* . . . b. *q*^{e}*lālâ* . . . *lô*
q l g l *q l l*
ôl ôl *lô*

In particular there is an 'indisputable play on words between *qwl* and *qllh*'.[1] This pinpoints the irony of the proverb: the voice (*qwl*) is not a blessing but a curse (*qllh*). The phrase *babbōqer haškêm* picks up the /o/ vowel of the preceding *b*^{e}*qôl gādôl* with *babbōqer* and has the only other sibilant /š / in the proverb to anticipate the verb *tēḥāšēb* in the next colon.

Finally, there is one more arrangement of sounds that should be pointed out. A chiasmus of vowel sounds is formed by four words in the first colon:

a. *m*^{e}*bārēk* . . . *gādôl* *babbōqer haškêm*
ā ē ā ô a ō a ê

In the second colon the /a, e/ assonance of the first colon is reversed and placed between an /a, o/ motif, also from the first colon.

b. *qelālâ tēḥāšēb lô*
â ē ā ô

These intertwined patterns tie all the phrases of the proverb together.

It is clear, then, that both *bqwl gdwl* and *bbqr hškym* have enough phonic qualities to indicate that they really belong in the proverb. Delitzsch's suggestion, that the unusual length of the proverb is intentional, can be accepted on the basis of the sound patterns. At the same time and for the same reason they could be variants as Scott proposed. Proposals to delete one or the other of them do not seem expedient any longer. At least that much certainty can be brought to an understanding of this proverb by an analysis of its sounds.

1. Boström, *Paronomasi*, p. 81.

Proverbs 15.12. This proverb is an example of how the sound of just one consonant, /l/, can be used to great effect.

a. *lō' ye'ehab lēṣ hôkēaḥ lô* The scoffer does not like anyone rebuking him;
b. *'el ḥakāmîm lō' yēlēk* to the wise he will not go.

The /l/ appears with either /e/ or /o/ vowels, the pair alternating in a regular alliterative motif:

a. *lō' y'hb lēṣ hwkḥ lô* b. *'el ḥkmym lō' yēlēk*
lō lē lô *el lō ēlē*

The /l, o/ sequence is associated with the negative attitude of the *lēṣ*, while the /l, e/ sequence joins words referring to the antipathy of the *lēṣ* for the wise, to (*'el*) whom he will not go (*yēlēk*). This sound pattern, in other words, draws attention to the basic attitudes of the *lēṣ* being described by the proverb.[1]

But each colon has a separate sound pattern of its own. The first colon revolves around the alternating consonance of /l/ and /h/, the second, around /l/ and /k/:

a. *lō' ye'ehab lēṣ hôkēaḥ lô* b. *'el ḥakāmîm lō' yēlēk*
lō h l hô lô *el k l ēlēk*

Further cohesion is lent to these patterns by the fact that each colon begins and ends on its own distinctive sound: /lō/ in the first and /el/ in the second. The cola themselves are linked to each other chiastically, for the two verbal phrases in each have the same /lō', ye/ pattern, while *hôkēaḥ lô* and *'el ḥakāmîm* share the sequence /k, ḥ, l/.

a. *lō' ye'ehab lēṣ hôkēaḥ lô* b. *'el ḥakāmîm lō' yēlēk*
lō' ye' k ḥ l *l ḥ k lō' yē*

The /k, h, l/ sequence of the first colon is completely reversed in the second—a smaller chiasmus mirroring the structural chiasmus of the whole.[2] This latter sound pattern illustrates what the proverb is *suggesting*: that the wise are the ones who would reprove the *lēṣ*. The chiasmus brings *ḥakāmîm* into relationship with the first colon and *hôkēaḥ lô* into association with the second. The sound pattern in other words provides the middle term between the two cola: the wiser *are*

1. *BHS* suggests 'frt l *'et*' in place of *'el*. This would surely weaken the sound pattern.
2. Boström, *Paronomasi*, p. 152.

the reprovers. And so there is a parallelism which can be formulated as follows:

a.	*lō' ye'ᵉhab*	*lēṣ*	*hôkēaḥ lô*
	A	B	C
b.	*'el ḥᵃkāmîm*		*lō' yēlēk*
	C′		A′

Thus, the sound patterning and meaning work closely together in this proverb.

There is a way of testing these sound patterns. In individual proverbs the presence and significance of certain sound patterns can often be illustrated by substituting words in the saying or changing the word order without affecting the meaning at all. The effect of these manipulations on the sounds of the proverb can then be measured against the MT version of the proverb and the critical value of the original sound structure thereby estimated. If the verb *yiśnā'*, for instance, were substituted for *lō' ye'ᵉhab* in the first colon and the noun *tôkēḥâ* were put in the place of *hôkēaḥ lô*, the relationship among the various parts of the saying would change drastically, even though the meaning of the first colon would remain intact.

* *yiśnā' lēṣ tôkēḥâ*	The scoffer hates rebuke;
'el ḥᵃkāmîm lō' yēlēk	to the wise he will not go.

Sound patterns involving /l/ and /o/ would all but disappear, as would the motifs binding the two cola together. The close connection between the 'rebuke' and *'el ḥᵃkāmîm*, so significant for understanding the proverb, would also be less clear. The semantic connection between the two cola, therefore, would be weakened without the sound structure to reinforce it. The hypothetical proverb appears more like two *separate* statements about the *lēṣ*, rather than one statement made up of two complementary parts. The power of the original saying in Prov. 15.12 is all the more impressive by the contrast.

Proverbs 25.28. Sounds help to join what is being compared in this proverb.

a.	*'îr pᵉrûṣâ 'ên ḥômâ*	An open city without a wall—
b.	*'îš 'ᵃšer 'ên ma'ṣār lᵉrûḥô*	a man who has no control over his spirit.

First of all, there is a similar structure in each colon: the image (*'îr*) plus an *'ên* clause; that to which the image is compared (*'îš*) plus an *'ên* clause. The use of the *'ᵃšer*, furthermore, gives the phrase *'îš 'ᵃšer* a length comparable to that of the image, *'îr pᵉrûṣâ*, and also picks up the /r, (ṣ, š)/ sequence of the latter, complemented by the /î/ vowel assonance in *'îr* and *'îš*. Thus, a full sequence is involved /î, r, (ṣ, š)/, in which the /r/ is repeated twice in the first colon and a sibilant twice in the second colon.

a.	*'îr pᵉrûṣâ 'ên ḥômâ* *îr r ṣ ên*	b.	*'îš 'ᵃšer 'ên ma'ṣār lᵉrûḥô* *îš š r ên*

The proverb centers on the comparison between 'the defenseless city' (colon a) and 'the man without control' (colon b). The two phrases which convey this theme (*pᵉrûṣâ 'ên ḥômâ* and *'ên ma'ṣār lᵉrûḥô*) are highlighted and given emphasis by sound patterning. Thus, the /rû/ syllable of *pᵉrûṣâ*, and the /ḥô/ of *ḥômâ* are both found in *lᵉrûḥô*. In addition, the /', r/ sequence of *'îr* is found in *ma'ṣār* and the /r, ṣ/ sequence of *pᵉrûṣâ* is also repeated chiastically in *ma'ṣār*.[1]

a.	*'îr pᵉrûṣâ 'ên ḥômâ* *' r rûṣ ḥô*	b.	*'îš 'ᵃšer 'ên ma'ṣār lᵉrûḥô* *'ṣ r rûḥô*

After close analysis it is clear that *rûḥô* was chosen, not merely for reasons of proper psychology,[2] but because it provides two key sounds, /rû/ and /ḥô/, which connect to the picture in the first colon. The proverbial metaphor has unity of sound and sense.

Proverbs 23.1-3. The sound patterns described so far have been drawn from only the two-cola proverbs, the couplets, which make up the bulk of the material in chs. 10–29. But there are sayings longer than the couplet format. The sound patterns here are worth studying briefly to see how the techniques uncovered so far apply in these longer pieces. One such saying is Prov. 23.1-3.

1a.	*kî tēšēb lilḥôm 'et môšēl*	When you sit down to eat with a ruler,
1b.	*bîn tābîn 'et 'ᵃšer lᵉpānêkā*	consider attentively who is before you,[3]

1. Boström, *Paronomasi*, p. 74.
2. Delitzsch, *Biblical Commentary*, VI.2, p. 173.
3. A problem with this verse is whether *'et 'ᵃšer lᵉpānêkā* refers to the ruler or to the food. Here I treat the phrase as referring to the ruler (also Toy, *A Critical Commentary*, p. 428) especially because of the proximity of this phrase to *'et môšēl* in the previous colon. The setting being emphasized in this passage, as well as in

2a	*wᵉśamtā śakkîn bᵉlōʿekā*	and put a knife to your throat
2b.	*ʾim baʿal nepeš ʾāttâ*	if you have a big appetite;
3a.	*ʾal titʾāw lᵉmaṭʿammôtāy w*	don't long for his delicacies,
3b.	*wᵉhûʾ leḥem kᵉzābîm*	for it is deceptive food.

The sound patterning in these lines is quite marked and in what follows its most noteworthy features will be presented first verse by verse. The pattern for colon 1a is based primarily on sounds echoing the words *tēšēb* and *môšēl*.

1a. *kî tēšēb lilḥôm ʾet môšēl*
t šē t šē
l l ôm mô l

The motif /t, šē/ links *tēšēb* and *ʾet môšēl*, while the motif /m, ô, l/ joins *môšēl* and *lilḥôm*. The next colon repeats the sounds of its verb *tābîn*.

1b. *bîn tābîn ʾet ʾᵃšer lᵉpānêkā*
b n t b n t p n

There are, finally, some motifs which both of these cola share. The first half of each colon has a motif using the sounds /î, t, b/. The second half of each colon has the exact same sequence in each, /t, š, l/.

1a. *kî tēšēb llḥwm* *ʾt mwšl*
î t b *t šl*
1b. *bîn tābîn* *ʾt ʾšr lpnyk*
bî t bî *t š l*

The principal patterns for the second verse are sibilants and /k/, plus the consonance between the words *blʿk* and *bʿl*, which involves a wordplay between them.

2a. *wśmt śkyn blʿk* 2b *ʾm bʿl npš ʾth*
ś ś *š*
k k
blʿ *bʿl*

Concerning the relationship between *blʿk*, 'your throat', and *bʿl npš*, 'owner of an appetite', Dahood remarks how the etymological meaning

parallel Egyptian texts (*Amen-em-opet* 23.13-18; *ANET*, p. 424; and *Ptah-Hotep*, 120-40; *ANET*, p. 412), is that of a meal in the presence of a great man or leader. It is possible, however, that the ambiguity of the phrase is intentional, referring to both the ruler and his food.

of *npš* as 'throat' creates a clever, ironic reprise from second colon (2b) to first (2a).[1] In verse 3 there is a repetitive sound pattern in the first colon involving the alliteration of /l, (t, ṭ), ā(y)w/. Another sequence, /l, m, m/, links the first colon with the second.

3a.	*'l tit'āw lmṭ'mwtāyw*	3b.	*whw' lḥm kzbym*
	l t t āw l ṭ tāy w		
	lm m		*l m m*

Interlinear sound patterning begins with colon 2a, which echoes colon 1b by the /în/ sound of *śakkîn* and the words *bîn tābîn*. The /k/ of *śakkîn* (2a) also picks up the /k/ of *kî* (1a) and *lpnyk* (1b). The words *lpnyk* (1b) and *bl'k* (2a) also share some consonance, /l, (p, b), k/, which prepares the listener for the *bl'k–b'l* wordplay.

1a.	*kî tšb llḥwm 't mwšl*		
	k		
1b.	*bîn tābîn 't 'šr lpnyk*	2a.	*wśmt śakkîn bl'k*
	k		*kk k*
	în în		*în*
	lp k		*bl k*

Interlinear euphony through the rest of the proverb includes, first of all, the series /t (ṭ)/ beginning at the end of colon 2b with *'th* and continuing into the first part of the third verse (3a):

2b.	*. . . 'th.*	3a.	*'l tt'w lmṭ'mwtyw*
	t		*tt ṭ t*

Then there is the phonic inclusion formed by the consonant sequence /l, ḥ, m/ contained in *lilḥôm* of the first colon (1a) and *leḥem* of the last. The final word of the proverb, *k*^{e}*zābîm*, adds one last /k/ sound after *lpnyk* (1b) and *bl'k* (2a). All in all this longer proverb demonstrates a consistent pattern of euphony, mainly comprised of distinct patterning between the cola of a line, and between lines.

1. M. Dahood, *Proverbs and Northwest Semitic Philology* (Rome: Pontificium Institutum Biblicum, 1963), p. 47.

Chapter 3

LINKING SOUND PATTERNS

Introduction

Chapter 2 dealt with common types of sound patterning, such as consonance, assonance and alliteration, in various configurations called motifs, which represent the many ways sounds can repeat in a line of Hebrew verse. The analysis of these motifs is useful for suggesting in an orderly way the richness and variety of the sound patterns in a line or so of poetry. The sometimes meticulous analysis of these patterns can bring the poetic structure and meaning into clearer focus and even be an aid to text criticism, as several examples in the previous chapter illustrated. But particular configurations or 'models' of sound patterns have limits. The particular categories used nearly always overlap and are never meant to be exhaustive. These qualifications should be borne in mind as the investigation proceeds.

In this chapter a linking sound pattern will be illustrated. This type of pattern joins words in a proverb sequentially, that is, one word is linked to a second by sound, and the second word in turn is linked to a third, but not always by the same sounds as in the preceding link. Often these sequential links join words one after another, but not always. Usually, too, this phonic linking is limited to one colon, or different patterns are found in each colon. Occasionally, however, the pattern continues from the first colon into the second. These links are usually not the only sound patterns in the proverb, but one or more patterns are interwoven with it. Thus, for example, the Latin phrase *per aspera ad astra*[1] has three phonic links:

1. Stevenson (*The Home Book of Proverbs*, p. 2208) gives this history of the saying. Suggested either by Virgil or Seneca the saying has another form: *Ad astra per ardua*. Another proverb is similar to it: *Per angusta ad augusta*. The original proverb was switched to read *Ad astra per aspera* when it was adopted as the state motto of Kansas in 1861.

per aspera ad astra
p r p r
ad a t
as ra as ra

And in the following English proverb, besides a consonant series in /s/, two linking patterns enhance the sound structure:

Speech is silvern, silence is golden
s s s s s
s l n s l n
len l en

These linking sound patterns may be somewhat less obvious at first hearing than a sequence of the same consonants repeated throughout the entire verse. But these links provide the artist with more variety, since he can choose different sequences of sound to give a line euphonic unity. At this juncture it is well to recall one critic's answer to the question of whether some of the sounds which occur just two or three times can have such an effect:

> However effective is the emphasis on repetition in poetry, the sound texture is still far from being confined to numerical contrivances, and a phoneme that appears only once, but in a key word, in a pertinent position, against a contrastive background, may acquire a striking significance. As painters used to say, 'Un kilo de vert n'est pas plus vert qu'un demi kilo'.[1]

Nor need the composer have been conscious of each and every sound effect in order to justify its existence. Sounds, even without conscious effort, naturally attract like sounds and can still contribute to the structure of the saying.[2] What is to be avoided is finding patterns in quite random and non-significant sounds.[3]

Texts

Proverbs 15.31. This proverb is a well-formed pattern of phonic links. Alliteration provides strong links between the words of the saying.

1. Jakobson, 'Closing Statement', pp. 373-74.
2. Masson, 'Sound in Poetry', p. 785; W.F. Holladay, 'Form and Word-Play in David's Lament over Saul and Jonathan', *VT* 20 (1970), p. 160.
3. Holladay, 'Form and Word-Play', p. 160.

a. *'ōzen šōma'at tôkaḥat ḥayyîm*	One with ear attentive to life-giving correction
b. *b*^{e}*qereb ḥ*^{a}*kāmîm tālîn*	will dwell among the wise.

A sequence of /o/ vowels and sibilants, /o, (z, š)/, links *'ōzen* to *šōma'at*, then *šōma'at* is linked to *tôkaḥat* by the /o, a, (at, t)/ sequence in each.[1] Finally the sequence /t, ḥ/ links *tôkaḥat* and *ḥayyîm*.

a. *'ōzen šōma'at tôkaḥat ḥayyîm*
ōz šō
ō a at ô a at
t t ḥ t ḥ

Admittedly this analysis is somewhat complicated by the different origins and lengths of these MT /o/ vowels.

In the second colon the consonance of /q/ and /k/ links *bqrb* with *ḥkmym* and the latter, picking up the /a, im/ assonance in *ḥayyîm*, is tied to *tālîn* by the same vowel rhyme.

b. *bqrb ḥ*^{a}*kāmîm tālîn*
q k
ā îm ā în

This proverb is one sentence composed of a subject (the first colon) and a predicate (the second colon); the linking sound patterns complement this structure by joining the words, one to the next, and by this vehicle of sound, carry the listener inevitably from beginning to conclusion.

One last sound pattern can be pointed out. Consonance helps provide an echo between the end of the first colon and the end of the second. The relationship involves the phrases *tôkaḥat ḥayyîm* and *ḥ*^{a}*kāmîm tālîn*.

a. *'zn šm't twkḥt ḥayyîm* b. *bqrb ḥkmîm tlîn*
t kḥt ḥ îm *ḥkmîm t în*

Such sound patterning knits the cola even more closely together and calls attention to the meaning: the *tôkaḥat* which leads to *ḥayyîm* enables one to live among the *ḥ*^{a}*kāmîm* because the *ḥ*^{a}*kāmîm* are its source.

1. However the feminine endings *-a't* and *-aḥt* were pronounced, the voweling was almost certainly identical.

Proverbs 29.12. Another well-developed example of a linking sound pattern can be found in this proverb.

a.	*mōšēl maqšîb 'al d^e bar šāqer*	A ruler attentive to deceptive talk—
b.	*kol m^e šār^e tāyw r^e šā'îm*	all his ministers are wicked.

In this proverb the simple association of the first colon with the second without the conjunction implies that the ministers' mores are consequent upon the ruler's.[1] But the proverb states this truism, not in a provisional form—'if a ruler is attentive to deceptive talk, then his ministers will become wicked'—but emphatically by simply stating deed and consequence together. Linking sound patterns emphasize this progression from condition to consequence. A /m, š / motif binds the words in the opening phrase *mšl mqšyb*. The sequence plus /r/ joins the last two words: *mšrtyw* and *rš'ym*. Another motif, /(q, k), š/, links the descriptive words *mqšyb* and *šqr* from the first colon with *kl mšrtyw* of the second. Some consonance with /l, b/ and /r/ completes the phonic picture of this proverb.

```
a. mšl mqšyb 'l dbr šqr        b. kl mšrtyw rš'ym
   mš  m  š                          mšr     rš  m
         qš         šq            k   š
     l       b  l  b
                  r    r
```

Proverbs 17.8. Linking patterns appear in each colon of this proverb.

a.	*'eben ḥēn haššōḥad b^e 'ênê b^e 'ālāyw*	The bribe is a lucky stone in the eyes of its bestower,
b.	*'el kol 'ašer yipneh yaśkîl*	everywhere he turns he succeeds.

In the first colon, the motif /b, n/ joins *'bn* and *b'yny*, while the /b, '/ sequence of *b'yny* links it to the following word, *b'lyw*. In addition, /n/ joins *'bn* and *ḥn*, and the /ḥ/ of *ḥn* repeats in the next word *hšḥd*.

```
a. 'bn ḥn hšḥd b'yny b'lyw
    bn          b  n
     n  n
        ḥ   ḥ
                b'    b'
```

1. Toy, *A Critical Commentary*, p. 510.

The second colon has a /l/ consonance and the sequence /k, l/ of *kl* is repeated in the verb *yśkyl.*

b. *'l kl 'šr ypnh yśkyl*
l l l
kl k l

Proverbs 11.21.

a. *yād lᵉyād lō' yinnāqeh rā'*	Assuredly the wicked person will not go unpunished,
b. *wᵉzera' ṣaddîqîm nimlāṭ*	but the company of the righteous will escape.

The first colon has a linking pattern of consonants for the first two words, involving the sequence /y, d, l/ and it is echoed again by the initial /y/ of the verb.

a. *yād lᵉyād lō' yinnāqeh rā'*
y d l y d l y

The second colon connects each successive word by different 'links'. The first 'link' is with sibilants, the second uses a motif of /m/ and dentals, /(d, ṭ), m/, which bind the words chiastically.

b. *wzr' ṣdyqym nmlṭ*
z ṣ
d m m ṭ

The whole, furthermore, is held together by another chiastic sound pattern. The /l, d/ consonance of the second word *lᵉyād* is echoed by the /l, ṭ/ of *nimlāṭ* at the end of the saying; the final letters of the first colon, *r'*, are a link to the first word of the second colon, *wᵉzera'*; and the motif /n, q/ of *ynqh* is found again in the words *ṣdyqym nmlṭ*. The chiastic configuration is formed in this way:

a. *yd lyd l' ynqh r'*	b. *wzr' ṣdyqym nmlṭ*
l d nq r'	*r' q n lṭ*
A B C	C′ B′ A′

Proverbs 15.29. A linking sound pattern is found almost exclusively in the second colon here.

a. *rāḥôq* YHWH *mērᵉšā'îm*	The Lord is far away from the wicked,
ûtᵉpillat ṣaddîqîm yišmā'	but he hears the prayer of the just.

In the second colon dental consonance is quite marked in the first two words. This dental sound forges a link between those two words. But there are no dentals in *yišmā'*. Rather, the link between it and the preceding word is formed by a tightening sequence of sibilants and /m/. To illustrate the pattern:

b. *wtplt ṣdyqym yšm'*
t t d
ṣ m šm

In addition, the pattern of short and long /i/ vowels throughout the colon complements the linking consonantal sounds. In the first colon, on the other hand, the only strong sound pattern between any of the words is the /r/ of *rḥwq* and *mrš'ym*.

A different, but striking phonic pattern in the proverb is the alliteration between the last words in each colon, *mēr*^{e}*šā'îm* and *yišmā'*. Not only is there a repetition of /a/ and /i/ vowels in each word, but there is also a consonantal sequence /š, ', m/ in each.

a. . . . *mēr*^{e}*šā'îm* b. . . . *yišmā'*
šā'îm *išmā'*

Thus, although the sound patterning and sense keep the cola distinct, this alliteration forges an almost ironic bond between the cola since it emphasizes the thematic contrast: the verb *yišmā'* expresses what the *r*^{e}*šā'îm* do not have —God's ear.

Proverbs 14.23. This saying also has a linking sound pattern only in the second colon.

a. *b*^{e}*kol 'eṣeb yihyeh môtār*	In all labor there is profit,
b. *ûd*^{e}*bar ś*^{e}*pātayim 'ak l*^{e}*maḥsôr*	but the chatter of lips leads only to poverty.

The dental and labial pair /d, b/ from *d*^{e}*bar* is echoed in reverse order in the following word, *ś*^{e}*pātayim*, by the dental and labial pair /p, t/. And the sequence /m, (ś, s), r/ of the last word, *maḥsôr*, is echoed, also in reverse order, in the first phrase of the colon.

b. *wdbr śptym 'k lmḥswr*
db pt
r ś m m s r

The phonic 'links' tie 'chattering lips' and 'poverty' together.

But this linking sound pattern only complements other patterns found in the proverb. The first colon shares a sound pattern with the second colon based on a /b, (ṣ, ś), (b, p)/ consonantal motif found in the first two words of each colon:

a. *bkl ʿṣb yhyh mwtr*   b. *wdbr śptym ʾk lmḥswr*
b ṣb   *b śp*

And the last words in each colon are not only the key words,[1] but also the strongest bond between the cola because of their final position in each colon, the semantic antithesis between them, and the alliteration. The consonants form the same pattern, but the vowels are chiastic in order:

a. . . . *môtār*   b. . . . *maḥsôr*
mô ār   *ma ôr*

The sounds alone of *môtār* and *maḥsôr* make them a natural, contrasting pair. Indeed, they appear in other proverbs involving a contrast between 'gain' and 'loss', such as Prov. 21.5, which will be reviewed next.

Proverbs 21.5. Not only does this proverb share a marked alliteration with *môtār* and *maḥsôr*, but it also utilizes linking sound patterns which carry through both cola.

a.	*maḥšᵉbôt ḥārûṣ ʾak lᵉmôtār*	The plans of the diligent lead only to plenty,
b.	*wᵉkol ʾāṣ ʾak lᵉmaḥsôr*	but all who are hasty head for poverty.

The linking patterns can be seen when diagrammed, the first colon appearing as follows:

a. *mḥšbôt ḥrwṣ ʾk lmôtr*
ḥš ḥ ṣ
m ôt r môtr

The second colon has these phonic links:

b. *wkl ʾṣ ʾk lmḥswr*
kl k l
ṣ s

Thus, each colon has its own individual sound pattern.

But another linking pattern begins in the first colon and is carried through to the second. This is a consonant motif, /k, l/, linking *ʾk*

1. Delitzsch, *Biblical Commentary*, VI.1, p. 306.

lmwtr of the first colon with *kl* and *'k lmḥswr* of the second colon.

a. . . . *'k lmwtr* b. *wkl 'ṣ 'k lmḥswr*
k l *kl* *k l*

Finally, the alliteration between the two *'ak* phrases with the words *môṭār* and *maḥsôr* is very strong:

a. . . . *-ṣ 'ak lᵉmô -ār*
b. . . . *-ṣ 'ak lᵉma -ôr*

These sound patterns especially highlight the perfect antithesis being expressed.

Proverbs 21.8. This proverb has a word whose meaning must be derived almost totally from the context.

a.	*hᵃpakpak derek 'îš wāzār*	Crooked is the way of the guilty man,
b.	*wᵉzak yāšār po'ᵒlô*	but as for the innocent man, his conduct is upright.

The meaning of *wāzār* at the end of the first colon is uncertain. Consequently, some emend the phrase to *'îš kāzāb*, 'a liar'.[1] Driver rewrites the whole colon, *'îš hᵃpakpak darkô zār*, and translates it, 'A man crooked of his way is false'.[2] But such changes ignore the linking sound pattern which clearly aligns *wāzār* by alliteration with the following word *wᵉzak*. In fact, its close phonic association with *wᵉzak* and the antithetic tone of the proverb would suggest that *wāzār* should be explained in antithesis to *wᵉzak*. As Boström remarks, '*wzr* seems explicable only from an external accord with *wzk*'.[3] If this is the case, then, *wāzār*, as the antithesis of 'innocent', should have a meaning like 'sinner', 'criminal', 'guilty' or 'false'. Some have suggested an Arabic verbal cognate, *wazara*. Its fundamental sense, however, is 'carry (a load)', and only in a particular context does it mean 'be guilt-laden'.[4] It is to be noted that the MT form defended here is contrary to the norm for west Semitic where initial /w/ has switched to /y/. That may make *wāzār* an archaizing, learned or dialectal form coined by the proverb maker for the sake of the sound patterning.

1. *BHS*; Scott, *Proverbs*, p. 123, n. c; Gemser, *Sprüche*, p. 81.
2. G.R. Driver, 'Problems in the Hebrew Text of Proverbs', *Bib* 32 (1951), p. 185.
3. Boström, *Paronomasi*, p. 184.
4. *HALAT*, p. 249.

Further confirmation for leaving *wāzār* as it is comes from the sound patterns in the proverb as a whole. The proverb pivots on the sounds of the consonants in *wāzār w*^{e}*zak*. First of all, the end of the first colon is echoed by the sounds at the beginning of the second:

a. . . . *'yš wzr* b. *wzk yšr* . . .
š wzr *wz šr*

This linkage is heavy with /a/ vowels as well. There is an additional linking consonance in which the /k/ of *hpkpk drk* is picked up by *wzk*, and the /r/ of *drk* is echoed by *wzr* and *yšr*.

a. *hpkpk drk 'yš wzr* b. *wzk yšr p'lw*
k k k *k*
r r *r*

In several ways, then, *wāzār w*^{e}*zak* both link and contain in themselves all the important sounds of the proverb. One final pattern can be mentioned which chiastically counterbalances the strong influence of *wāzār w*^{e}*zak*. This is the repetition of /p/ from *hpkpk* to *p'lw*, which links beginning and end of the proverb. Any attempts at textual emendation of this proverb will have to take into serious consideration all these prominent sound patterns.

Proverbs 11.4. Two different patterns of linking sounds unify each colon of this saying.

a. *lō' yô'îl hôn b*^{e}*yôm 'ebrâ*	Wealth gives no advantage on the day of fury,
b. *ûṣ*^{e}*dāqâ taṣṣîl mimmawet*	but virtue saves from death.

The consonant /l/ links the first two words, the nasals /n/ and /m/ the third and fourth words, and /b/ the last two words.

a. *l' yw'yl hwn bywm 'brh*
l l
n m
b b

The first colon is also strong in /o/ vowels, which disappear in the second half of the saying. Dentals are the strongest links in the second colon, and then sibilants:

b. *wṣdqh tṣyl mmwt*
ṣ ṣ
d t t

But the proverb itself is unified around a chiastic sound pattern which joins the cola together: an /â/ rhyme joins the last word of the first colon with the first word of the second colon; and a final /îl/ syllable appears in both verbs.

a.	*l' yô'îl hwn bywm 'ebrâ*	b.	*ûṣ^e^dāqâ taṣṣîl mmwt*
	îl *â*		*â* *îl*

The chiasmus joins the key antitheses of the whole saying: 'has (no) advantage' and 'saves'; 'virtue' and what the lack of virtue leads to, 'the day of fury'.

Proverbs 16.31. This traditional wisdom statement joining virtue with long life is punctuated with dental sounds and also has linking sound patterns.

a.	*'ᵃṭeret tip'eret śêbâ*	A crown of glory is grey hair;
b.	*b^e^derek ṣ^e^dāqâ timmāṣē'*	it is gained by the path of virtue.

The first sound pattern is the series of dentals in both cola.

a.	*'ṭrt tp'rt śybh*	b.	*bdrk ṣdqh tmṣ'*
	ṭ t t *t*		*d* *d* *t*

There are exactly three words in each colon but the dentals are evenly distributed among them only in the second colon. There are two dentals in the first word of the first colon and two in the middle word. The third word, *śêbâ*, lacking any dental sound, stands apart from this consonant motif. This phonic contrast between *śêbâ* and the rest of the proverb highlights its uniqueness as the subject of both cola. There are two things said about *śêbâ*: it is 'a crown of glory' and 'it is gained by virtue'. Both of these phrases are joined by consonance. The word *śêbâ* itself, however, is given prominence by being centrally placed between both phrases.

The next sound pattern links just certain words in the proverb. A series of labials joins *tip'eret* and *śêbâ* with the first word of the second colon, *b^e^derek*. This latter word in turn is linked to *ṣ^e^dāqâ* by a /k, q/ consonance. Again, *ṣ^e^dāqâ* is joined to the last word, *timmāṣē'*, by /ṣ/.

a.	*'ṭrt tp'rt śybh*	b.	*bdrk ṣdqh tmṣ'*
	p *b*		*b*
			k *q*
			ṣ *ṣ*

In effect, the subpatterns link every word but the first. But another linking sound pattern balances this. It is the segholate alliteration, the /ere/ motif, which links the initial words of the first colon and then is echoed again in *b^e^derek* at the beginning of the second colon.

a. *ʿ^a^ṭeret tip'eret. . .* b. *b^e^derek. . .*

This alliteration is present no matter how the original final /a/ plus double consonants were pronounced in ancient Hebrew. Finally, to speak of assonance, the /śê/ syllable of *śêbâ* is echoed in the final syllable of *timmāṣē'*, which words also share an /e, a/ assonance:

a. . . . *śêbâ* b. *timmāṣē'*
ê â *ā ē*

There is also rhyme between the /a/ vowel of *śêbâ* and *ṣ^e^dāqâ*. Thus, while *śêbâ* is isolated in terms of the dental sounds, it is linked to those words by other sounds.

The importance of these sound patterns can hardly be overestimated. For example, the word order in Prov. 16.31 could be rearranged in the following way (while maintaining the same meaning as the MT version):

śêbâ ʿ^a^ṭeret tip'eret
timmāṣē' b^e^derek ṣ^e^dāqâ

The proverb would be following the normal word order for a Hebrew sentence in this case. But as a result of these changes the sense of anticipation, which was created by placing *śêbâ* in the prominent final position in the first colon, is lost and the dental sounds now follow each other quite monotonously without a break. The linking sound patterns, which utilized the labials /b/ and /p/ as well as the sibilant /ṣ/, are also broken: *śêbâ* is separated from *tip'eret*, and *timmāṣē'* from *ṣ^e^dāqâ*. Thus, a substantial part of the sound patterning is gone in this hypothetical version. Although the meaning of the words is the same, the striking mode of expression which is a hallmark of proverbial language is lost. A mere sentence remains, not a proverb.

Proverbs 22.10. This proverb provides an example of a linking sound pattern closely tied in with the semantic structure.

a.	*gārēš lēṣ w*^{e}*yēṣē' mādôn*	Drive out the arrogant man so that strife may go away,
b.	*w*^{e}*yišbōt dîn w*^{e}*qālôn*	and argument and scorn may cease.

The pattern in the first colon begins with the first three words and involves an /e/ vowel assonance associated with sibilants.

a.	*gārēš*	*lēṣ*	*w*^{e}*yēṣē'*	*mādôn*
	ēš	*ēṣ*	*ēṣē*	

Grammatically speaking, these sounds link an imperative (*gārēš*), and its object (*lēṣ*), with the first of two following indirect volitives (*w*^{e}*yēṣē'*), or, in semantic terms, cause ('drive out') with result ('strife goes away'). However, *mādôn* does not link with any of these words.

The second colon (the second indirect volitive, *w*^{e}*yišbōt*) is really an additional result of *gārēš* and further links become apparent, when the first two words of this colon are lined up next to *w*^{e}*yēṣē' mādôn* from the first colon.

a.	. . . *w*^{e}*yēṣē'*	*mādôn*	b.	*w*^{e}*yišbōt*	*dîn*	*w*^{e}*qālôn*
	w^e*y ṣ '*	*ād n*		*w*^{e}*y š*		*ā ôn*
		d n			*d n*	

The alliteration is striking. The two indirect volitives have a /wĕy/ plus sibilant sequence in common, and *mādôn* and *qālôn* have a feminine end rhyme /ā, ôn/. The /d, n/ of *mādôn* is also repeated in the word *dîn*.

Quite clearly, then, this proverb is built on a linking sound pattern with the *w*^{e}*yēṣē'* playing a pivotal role in joining the first part of the saying (cause) with the second (result):

Cause	/	Result				
gārēš lēṣ	/	*w*^{e}*yēṣē'*	*mādôn*	*w*^{e}*yišbōt*	*dîn*	*w*^{e}*qālôn*
ēš ēṣ	/	*ēṣē*				
		w^e*y ṣ*		*w*^{e}*y š*		
			d n		*d n*	
			ā ôn			*ā ôn*

The full phrase *w*^{e}*yēṣē' mādôn* prepares for the echoing sounds in the second colon. The recognition of this sound pattern renders suspect any emendation of the second colon of the MT to read (on the basis of the LXX):

wyšb bt dyn wyqlnw[1]	for when he sits in the law-court, he dishonors it.

Not only does this change destroy a perfectly normal Hebrew text, but it also completely ignores the heavy sound patterning. Such an emendation, therefore, can only appear to be very arbitrary. The error is surely in the Hebrew *Vorlage* of the LXX.[2]

1. This follows the suggestion of Driver, 'Problems', p. 186. P. de Lagarde (*Anmerkungen zur griechischen Übersetzung der Proverbien* [Leipzig: F.A. Brockhaus, 1863], p. 70) attributes the 'successful' accommodation of the first word of the MT to the LXX reading to Vogel (G.J.L. Vogel's notes to his 1769 printing of A. Schultens's *Proverbia Salomonis*).

2. A comparison of the MT with the Hebrew text reconstructed from the LXX illustrates this assertion.

MT:	*wyšbt*	*dyn wqlwn*
LXX Vorlage:	*wyšb*	*bt dyn wyqlnw*

First, there was a false word division (*bt* off the end of *wyšbt*) with dittography of the /b/. This error probably triggered the corruption of *wqlwn* to *wyqlnw*, an error involving the frequent *waw–yod* confusion, and the metathesis of /wn/.

Chapter 4

CORRELATION

Introduction

Chapter 2 introduced the study of sound patterns in Hebrew verse by analysing basic motifs or arrangements of sounds formed by assonance, consonance and alliteration. These motifs were simply loose configurations that provided some control over the material. A somewhat tighter category of sound patterning was presented in Chapter 3 with the linking sound pattern. Instead of looking for euphony in a line of verse by means of the same sequence of similar or identical sounds, this category illustrated how the line can often be viewed in terms of smaller and different sequences of sounds, which join various parts of a verse one after another.

The next sound pattern to be introduced is correlation, which is defined as 'indirect support of argument by related echoes'.[1] That is, the sounds of the word or words which are key to the meaning are echoed in various ways throughout the verse so as to subtly reinforce the sense. Notice how G.M. Hopkins carries over the sounds of 'grieving', a key theme in his poem *Spring and Fall: To A Young Child*, into the next verse, associating the grief phonically as well as semantically with its object, 'Goldengrove unleaving'.

Márgarét, áre you gríeving
rg r r gríeving
Over Goldengrove unleaving?
r g gr eaving?

By this means the poet can reiterate his theme while still advancing the thought; the sounds of 'grieving' are still heard, even as its cause is being mentioned. The use of such correlating sound patterns ties

1. Masson, 'Sound in Poetry', p. 785.

together important parts of the semantic structure of poetry as do, for instance, the verbs in these few lines from A.E. Housman's *To An Athlete Dying Young*:

The time you won your town the race
We chaired you through the market-place
ch r
Man and boy stood cheering by. . .
ch r

The /ch, r/ motif connects the 'chairing' with the 'cheering', joining by sound two parts of the description of the crowd honoring its hero. The end rhyme between 'race' and 'market-place' completes the picture by joining the celebration with its cause. With these two simple figures of sound the poet indirectly reinforces important elements in his description. A number of the Hebrew proverbs make good use of this kind of sound pattern.

Texts

Proverbs 19.17. In the first example the sound patterning is not heavy but it does correlate three significant words.

a.	*malwēh* YHWH *ḥônēn dāl*	Whoever has pity on the poor is a lender to God
b.	*ûg^{e}mūlô y^{e}šallem lô*	and he will repay him for his kind deed.

Besides the /l/ repetition throughout the proverb, a /m, l/ motif connects the key words *malwēh* and *g^{e}mūlô* at the beginning of each colon, and also *y^{e}šallem lô* in the second colon. Even more specifically, a /m, lô/ sequence is found at the beginning and end of the second colon: *g^{e}mūlô* and *y^{e}šallem lô*.

a. *malwēh* YHWH *ḥônēn dāl* b. *ûg^{e}mūlô y^{e}šallem lô*
m l *l* *m lô* *ll m lô*

These few sounds amply highlight the words which carry the theme of the proverb: the lender (*mlwh*) will be repaid (*yšlm*) for his deed (*gmlw*).

Proverbs 11.26. The opening sounds of this proverb are repeated at the beginning and end of the second colon.

a.	*mōnēa' bār yiqq^{e}būhû l^e'ôm*	The one who hoards grain people curse,
b.	*ûb^{e}rākâ l^{e}rō'š mašbîr*	but a blessing is for the head of the one who sells it!

The theme of the proverb revolves around *bār*, 'grain'. After the word is introduced in the first colon, its consonants appear again in *b*[e]*rākâ* and *mašbîr* of the second colon,[1] underlining the positive theme that the seller (*mšbyr*) of grain (*br*) is blessed (*brkh*). In addition, the phrase *mōnēa' bār* is picked up at the end of the proverb by the /m, b, r/ sequence in *mašbîr*, thus linking those antithetic personalities not only by sense but also by sound.

a. *mn' br yqbhw l'wm* b. *wbrkh lr'š mšbyr*
m br *br m b r*

The final colon has an additional sound pattern involving /b, r, š/:

b. *wbrkh lr'š mšbyr*
br r š šb r

These sounds emphasize that the *b*[e]*rākâ* belongs to the *rō'š mašbîr*.

Proverbs 22.7. The four key words are linked by the principal sound patterning in this proverb.

a. *'āšîr b*[e]*rāšîm yimšôl* The rich rule over the poor,
b. *w*[e]*'ebed lōweh l*[e]*'îš malweh* and the borrower is a slave to the lender.

In the first half of the saying the contrasting terms 'rich' and 'poor' are joined by the alliteration of /āšîr/ and /rāšî/ in *'šyr* and *bršym* respectively; in the second half, the 'borrower' and 'lender' are related by the repetition of the same verbal root, *lwy*.

a. *'āšîr b*[e]*rāšîm ymšwl* b. *w'bd lwh l'yš mlwh*
'āšîr rāšî *lwh lwh*

In addition to these correlating patterns the motif /š, m/ adds a further phonic association in the first colon, joining the words *bršym* and *ymšwl* in a chiastic sound pattern echoed by the /š/ in the first word.

a. *'šyr bršym ymšwl*
š š m mš

The consonant /l/ predominates in the second colon.

b. *w'bd lwh l'yš mlwh*
l l l

1. Boström, *Paronomasi*, p. 132.

The last word of the first colon and the last two words of the second are joined by a /m, š, l/ motif:

a.		b.
. . . *ymšwl*		. . . *l'yš mlwh*
mš l		*l š ml*

The use of the semantically redundant *l'yš* has the effect of recalling the verb *ymšwl*, something that would have been missed if the second colon had merely read:

w'bd lwh lmlwh

As it is, the phonic association suggests what the actual juxtaposition of the cola is also intended to convey—that the 'lender rules'.

Proverbs 21.24. In this saying just two words are connected by a correlation.

a.	*zēd yāhîr lēṣ š*^{e}*mô*	The insolent, haughty person—'scoffer' is his name,
b.	*'ôśeh b*^{e}*'ebrat zādôn*	the one who acts with excessive pride.

In the midst of this proverbial 'pile-up' of epithets, the most obvious sound correlation is the consonance between *zēd* and *zādôn*. This enhances the proverb's semantic emphasis by cognate repetition with the root *zd* at the beginning and end. Such a correlation, of course, doubly reinforces the primary theme of pride and also unifies the saying. The /ô/ assonance among *š*^{e}*mô*, *'ôśeh* and *zādôn* brings the definition of the second colon into relationship with 'his name' and the epithets in the first colon. A final cohesive force is the sibilant consonance in both cola. All the sound patterns appear as follows:

a. *zd yhyr lṣ šmô*	b. *'ôśh b'brt zdôn*
zd	*zd*
ô	*ô ô*
z ṣ š	*ś z*

Proverbs 16.10. This proverb emphasizes two words by a sound motif repeated throughout both cola. Each colon, moreover, has another distinct sound pattern.

a.	*qesem 'al śiptê melek*	An oracle is on the king's lips;
b.	*b*^{e}*mišpāṭ lō' yim'al pîw*	in judgment his mouth does not speak falsely.

A /m, l/ sequence appears twice in each colon connecting all the phrases and echoing the key word *mlk* and the character of his speech, *l’ ym‘l*, by sound. The sequence also provides a distinct bond between the cola.

a. *qsm ‘l śpty mlk*   b. *bmšpṭ l’ ym‘l pyw*
m l ml   *m l m l*

Consonance draws yet another relationship between words by joining opposite ends of each colon. The ‘lips of the king’ are linked with his ‘judgment’ by a motif /(ś, š), p, (t, ṭ), m/:

a. *qsm ‘l śpty mlk*   b. *bmšpṭ l’ ym‘l pyw*
śpt m   *mšpṭ*

Some of those same consonants are found in the other words of the proverb, but the tight clustering of these sounds occurs with the words ‘lips of the king’ and ‘judgment’. The ‘oracle’, on the other hand, and the verb of the second colon are joined by another pattern, /m, ‘, l/:

a. *qsm ‘l śpty mlk*   b. *bmšpṭ l’ ym‘l pyw*
m ‘l   *m‘l*

These ‘crisscrossing’ patterns reinforce the theme of the solemnity and importance of royal decrees: ‘oracle’ is linked to the statement ‘does not speak falsely’ and the phrase ‘the king’s lips’ is matched with the word ‘judgment’.

Lastly, each colon has a distinct pattern. The first colon has the motif /(q, k), (s, ś), m, l/:

a. *qsm ‘l śpty mlk*
qsm l ś mlk

The second colon has another pattern with the consonants /(b, p), m, l/:

b. *bmšpṭ l’ ym‘l pyw*
bm p l m l p

Each of these patterns accounts for consonants that did not play a role in joining the cola.

Proverbs 15.24. A small debate concerns the use of l^{e}*ma‘lâ*, ‘upward’, and *māṭṭâ*, ‘below’, in this proverb. The LXX does not read l^{e}*ma‘lâ* and *māṭṭâ* or, at least, does not translate them as ‘upward’ and 'below'.[1] On this basis McKane deletes the words as later glosses reflecting a more 'heavenly' religious view when such an opposition (upward–below) would seem to make more sense.[2] On the other hand, Barucq suggests understanding the proverb in the light of the affirmations contained in Pss. 16.9-11, 55.16, and 73.24, Eccl. 3.21, Gen. 37.35, and Num. 16.33.[3] The affinity between the Proverbs text and Deut. 28.13-14—the thesis of the two alternatives with the same vocabulary (*lm'lh lmṭh* and *swr*) to express it, and the same basic affirmation in each text about the 'way'—has long since been pointed out.[4] The way leading 'upward' need not necessarily indicate a conviction about a heavenly afterlife, but can simply be part of the expression which contrasts with 'Sheol below'. It is the way the proverb positively illustrates the assertion that the prudent person's path does not lead toward Sheol. 'Upward' and 'below' are in relation to Sheol alone, and do not need to be tied into a 'this world'/'other world' scheme. Besides, such alternatives and opposite expressions are part of the very style of Proverbs, especially evident in the innumerable contrasts involved in the sayings of chs. 10–15.

Relevant to this discussion is an analysis of the sound patterns in the proverb in which the letters /l/ and /m/ play an important role.

a.	*'oraḥ ḥayyîm l^ema'lâ l^emaśkîl*	The road of life is upward for the prudent person
b.	*l^ema'an sûr miššᵉ'ôl māṭṭâ*	so that he may turn away from Sheol below.

1. The LXX text is:

ὁδοὶ ζωῆς διανοήματα συνετοῦ,
ἵνα ἐκκλίνας ἐκ τοῦ ᾅδου σωθῇ.

The thoughts of the intelligent man are paths of life,
so that turned aside from Hades he might be saved.

2. McKane, *Proverbs*, pp. 234, 479-80. In this regard McKane on p. 479 is inexact in his citation of Barucq. Barucq (*Le livre*, p. 136, in a footnote to Prov. 15.24, which comments on the questions surrounding *lm'lh* and *mṭh*) writes: 'On y a parfois vu des gloses tardives. . .' McKane's remarks, apparently referring to this footnote, imply that Barucq is saying the Hebrew words 'should be regarded as additions. . .' Barucq, however, is quite open to seeing the disputed words as part of the text, as his commentary on p. 111 reveals.

3. Barucq, *Le livre*, p. 111.

4. A. Robert, 'Le Yahvisme de Prov x, 1–xxii, 16; xxv–xxix', *Mémorial Lagrange* (Paris: Gabalda, 1940), p. 167.

First of all, the relationship between ‘upward’ and ‘the prudent person’ is underscored by the /lĕma, l/ sequence in both words. Secondly, ‘Sheol’s’ connection with ‘downward’ is emphasized by the /m/ consonance between them both.

a. . . . l^{e}*ma‘lâ* l^{e}*maśkîl*
l^{e}*ma l* l^{e}*ma l*

b. . . . *mš’wl mṭh*
m m

There is more. The words l^{e}*ma‘lâ,* l^{e}*maśkîl* and l^{e}*ma‘an* are also related by the phonic repetition of the initial cluster /lĕma/, and the opening and concluding phrase of the second colon are bound together by a /l, ma/ sequence, a pattern which provides an echo of the /lĕma/ motif.

a. . . . l^{e}*ma‘lâ* l^{e}*maśkîl*
l^{e}*ma* l^{e}*ma*

b. l^{e}*ma‘an swr mš’wl māṭṭâ*
l^{e}*ma*
l ma l mā

These sounds prompt Boström to say, ‘The whole saying is so built up on the sounds of *lm* that the *BHK*’s questionable note for deleting *lm‘lh* and *mṭh* must be simply rejected’.[1] Such clear patterns of alliteration are strong evidence in favor of preserving the present Hebrew text of the saying.

Other complex sound patterns are visible. The words l^{e}*ma‘lâ* and l^{e}*ma‘an* are related on the basis of the alliteration of the /lĕma‘/ motif.[2] ‘Upwards’ and ‘below’ have an end rhyme in /â/; l^{e}*maśkîl* and *mišš*^{e}*’ôl* have in common a /m, (ś, š), l/ motif; and the /r/ in *sûr* could recall the /r/ of *’ōraḥ*.

a. *’rḥ ḥyym* l^{e}*ma‘lâ lmśkyl*
l^{e}*ma‘*
r â mś l

b. l^{e}*ma‘an swr mš’wl māṭṭâ*
l^{e}*ma‘*
r mš l â

The sounds of this proverb not only link words in sequence, but also relate the words from one colon to the other. Just as *’ōraḥ ḥayyîm* is grammatically and semantically attributed to the *maśkîl* in the first colon, the *maśkîl* is also associated with *sûr mišš*^{e}*’ôl* by

1. Boström, *Paronomasi*, p. 154. Gemser (*Sprüche*, p. 69) also warns that striking these words from the text would destroy the paronomasia of the saying.

2. Boström, *Paronomasi*, p. 154.

sounds in the second. The proverb is saying, in effect, that two things belong to the prudent person: 'the road to life' and 'the avoidance of Sheol'. The words *l^ema'lâ* and *māṭṭâ* point out this equation and the implied contrast invloved. The parallelism of the proverb appears this way:

a.	*'ōraḥ ḥayyîm*	*l^ema'lâ*	*l^emaśkîl*
	A	B	C
b.	*l^ema'an*	*sûr miššᵉ'ôl*	*māṭṭâ*
	D	A′	B′

The particle *l^ema'an* gives a balanced length to the second colon and helps reinforce the alliterative pattern. Otherwise, the proverb really pivots on the relationships of A–B and A′–B′ to C. Because of the sounds, the word *l^emaśkîl* holds the prominent, pivotal position at the end of the first colon, in the middle of the entire saying. It should be obvious from the detailed sound patterns that to change any of these words would risk disturbing the tight cohesion of the proverb.

Proverbs 25.13. The usefulness of a study of sound patterns as a corroborative argument for text criticism can be illustrated in this proverb.

a.	*k^eṣinnat šeleg b^eyôm qāṣî r*	Like the coolness of snow on a harvest day—
b.	*ṣîr ne'^emān l^ešōl^eḥāy w*	the faithful messenger to the ones who send him
c.	*w^enepeš 'ᵃdōnāyw yāšîb*	for he restores the spirit of his masters.

A chiastic sound pattern connects the first two cola of the proverb. It involves the syllable /ṣîr/ in *qāṣîr* and *ṣîr*, which joins the end of the first colon to the beginning of the next. The other link in the chiasmus is forged by the /šl/ consonance of *šlg* in the first colon and *lšlḥyw* in the second.[1]

a.	*kṣnt šlg bywm qāṣîr*		b.	*ṣîr n'mn lšlḥyw*	
	šl	*ṣîr*		*ṣîr*	*lšl*

This chiasmus effectively joins the key words of the image and what is compared with it. The pattern underlines the main point of the proverb: the *ṣyr* ('messenger') is *šlg* ('snow') on the *qṣyr* ('harvest day') for the *šlḥyw* ('ones who send him'). The first colon has an additional consonance of its own: the /kṣ/ motif of the first word *kṣnt*

1. Boström, *Paronomasi*, p. 76.

is echoed by the /qṣ/ of *qṣyr* at the end of the colon. The word *n'mn* of the second colon also reflects the /n/ of *kṣnt* and the /m/ of *bywm* in the first colon.

a.	*kṣnt*	*šlg*	*bywm*	*qṣyr*	b.	*ṣyr*	*n'mn*	*lšlḥyw*
	kṣ			*qṣ*				
	n		*m*				*n mn*	

The proverb concludes with an explanatory third colon which repeats some of the sounds of the previous two cola. A simple motif, /(s, š), i/, binds the first and last words of the proverb, *k*^{e}*ṣinnat* and *yāšîb*, with *qāṣîr* and *ṣîr*. All of the sibilant consonance throughout the proverb is re-echoed by *nepeš*, which, along with *'dnyw*, picks up the /n/ consonance of *kṣnt* and *n'mn*.

a.	*k*^{e}*ṣinnat*	*šlg*	*bywm*	*qāṣîr*	b.	*ṣîr*	*n'mn*	*lšlḥyw*	c.	*wnpš*	*'dnyw*	*yāšîb*
	ṣi	*š*		*ṣî*		*ṣî*		*š*		*š*		*šî*
	nn						*n n*			*n*	*n*	
										pš		*š b*

In addition the last colon has its own repeating sequence /n, (b, p), š/:

c.	*wnpš*	*'dnyw*	*yšyb*
	npš	*n*	*š b*

The preponderance of these sound patterns has to be kept in mind when considering the text-critical arguments for deleting the third colon as a gloss[1] or as a remnant of another proverb from which the other colon has disappeared.[2] The third colon's sound patterns, though not as overwhelming as the euphony of the first two cola, are real. The third colon has been phonically integrated with the other two cola and gives reason for caution in regarding it as a plus.

Proverbs 24.3-4. This quatrain emphasizes the imagery by repeating several letters of its key words throughout.

3a.	*b*^{e}*ḥokmâ yibbāneh bāyit*	By wisdom is a house built
3b.	*ûbitbûnâ yitkônān*	and by understanding it is made firm;
4a.	*ûb*^{e}*da'at ḥ*^{a}*dārîm yimmāl*^{e}*'û*	by knowledge are the rooms filled
4b.	*kol hôn yāqār w*^{e}*nā'îm*	with every precious and pleasing possession.

The phonically important words are *byt,* 'house', and the parallel

1. Toy, *A Critical Commentary*, p. 464, and Barucq, *Le livre*, p. 194.
2. Gemser, *Sprüche*, p. 91.

word pair *bnh* // *kwn*, 'build' // 'make firm'.[1] Thus /b/ is a particularly prominent sound, coming in the initial word of the first three cola and in each word of the first two cola except the last word *ytkwnn*. In the first colon the combination /b, t/, after its introduction in *byt* of 3a, is formed twice in 3b; the letters /b, n/, coming first in the verb *ybnh*, surface again in *wbtbwnh*.

3a.	*bḥkmh ybnh byt*	3b.	*wbtbwnh ytkwnn*
	b b t		*btb t*
	bn		*b n*
			n nn

Each colon of the first verse (24.3) also displays alliteration.[2]

3a. . . . *yibbāneh bāyit*
bā bā
3b. *ûbitbûnâ yitkônān*
it nâ it nā

The second verse (24.4) is less dramatic in its sound patterning. Various consonants link the words of the verse as follows:

4a. *wbd't ḥdrym yml'w*
d d
m m
4b. *kl hwn yqr wn'ym*
k q
n n

But these cola also echo the previous verse. The /b, t/ motif is found in *wbd't* of 4a, and the letters /k, n/ from the verb *ytkwnn* (3b) are repeated in the phrase *kl hwn* of 4b and echoed by the /q, n/ sequence of *yqr wn'ym* in the same colon. This /k, n/ pattern also involves the vowel /ô/.

3a.	. . . *byt*	3b.	*wbtbwnh ytkônn*
	b t		*btb t*
			kôn
4a.	*wbd't*. . .	4b.	*kl hôn yqr wn'ym*
	b t		
			k ôn q n

1. On this parallel word pair, see A.R. Ceresko, 'The Function of Chiasmus in Hebrew Poetry', *CBQ* 40 (1978), pp. 6-9.
2. Boström, *Paronomasi*, p. 198.

In summary, therefore, in this proverb about building houses, the sounds of the word for 'house', /b, t/, are used to 'build' the saying four times. Then the sounds for the verb 'to build', /b, n/, are used twice (in the first and second cola), and the consonants of the verb for making this structure 'firm, established, finished', /k, n/, are also used twice, once in 3b to make the structure firm and then in 4b to finish the project by furnishing the rooms.

Proverbs 20.9. In this proverb, which recalls the sentiments of Psalm 51 (especially vv. 5 and 7), the sounds echo not a particular word but a particular suffix affixed to nearly every word.

a.	*mî yō'mar zikkîtî libbî*	Who can say: 'I have made my heart clean;
b.	*ṭāhartî mēḥaṭṭā'tî*	I am cleansed from my sin'?

The assertion introduced by the rhetorical question portrays a self-centered and self-righteous person whose attitude is aptly expressed by the constant repetition of /i/ vowels. For it is the /i/ vowel that characterizes the separated pronoun and suffix of the first person singular in Hebrew. So, in effect, the proverb is repeatedly saying: 'me. . . me. . . me!' There is variety in the way these sounds are used too. The first colon has a multiplicity of /i/ vowels and only one /tî/ suffix, whereas the second colon, utilizing the /tî/ suffix and the letter /ṭ/, produces the motif /ṭ, tî/.

a.	*mî yō'mar zikkîtî libbî*	b.	*ṭāhartî mēḥaṭṭā'tî*
	î i îtî i î		*ṭ tî ṭṭ tî*

The whole combination of sounds ultimately builds up to a climax in 'my sin'. . . *zikkîtî*. . . *ṭāhartî mēḥaṭṭā'tî*. In addition, there are smaller phonic units. The first phrase, *mî yō'mar*, is linked by a /m/ consonance and the second, *zikkîtî libbî*, by /i/ assonance. The second colon has the /t, ṭ/ sequence already noted; and the /m/ of *mēḥaṭṭā'tî* and the /r/ of *ṭāhartî* recall the same sounds in the first colon:

a.	*my y'mr. . .*	b.	*ṭhrty mḥṭ'ty*
	m mr		*r m*

Chapter 5

TAGGING SOUND PATTERNS (1)

Introduction

Having reviewed in previous chapters the common phonic motifs and linking sound patterns, which deal, primarily, with basic sound structures in a verse, the investigation turned in Chapter 4 to sound patterns, which principally underscore key words in a proverb. Correlation referred to phonic patterns based on the sounds of only certain words that were important to the meaning of the verse. The next types of sound pattern are related to the syntactical units in a line of verse and in this way underscore the thought.

These are called tagging patterns of sound and are defined as 'punctuation of syntax or thought by sounds'.[1] By building themselves on the basis of syntactical or grammatical units, these sound patterns tag or mark off those units by phonic sequences and so indicate the building blocks of the thought itself. They differ from correlation by being more than an echo of certain key sounds; they represent by sound the progression of the thought itself. In the following line from W. Owen's poem, *Anthem for Doomed Youth*, for instance, the primary sound pattern clearly tags the metaphor by the repetition of the /p, l, r/ sequence:[2]

The pallor of girls' brows shall be their pall
p ll r   r p ll

Grammatical units can also be delineated by sound, as in the following proverb:

Spare the rod and spoil the child.
sp   d   sp   d

1. Masson, 'Sound in Poetry', p. 785.
2. Masson, 'Sound in Poetry', p. 785.

Each half of the proverb is marked by a /sp, d/ sequence. This is not to presume that there are no other sound patterns in the proverb but merely to point out the nature of the primary phonic figure. In fact, in this particular saying, the first half is marked by a consonance in /r/ and the second half by one in /l/.

These tagging sequences can, in fact, be more elaborate, as in this saying:

The sharper the blast, the shorter 'twill last.
the sh r er last the sh r er last

It should be noted that the effectiveness of this kind of sound pattern increases the more the repetition is based on the same sounds either in the same order or in chiasmus. In Gen. 27.36, the sequence /b, k, r, tî/, plus the repetition of the verb *lqḥ*, effectively supports the semantic chiasmus and inclusion:[1]

't bkrtî lqḥ whnh 'th lqḥ brktî
bkrtî lqḥ lqḥ brktî

Another famous example of this tagging sound pattern is also from Genesis (9.6):

špk dm h'dm b'dm dmw yšpk
špk dm 'dm 'dm dm špk

The sound patterns and word repetition here touch just about every consonant. The chiastic arrangement of the words (and therefore, too, of the sounds) not only delineates each half of the verse, but also phonically represents the reversal of fortune described. The verse begins with *špk* and concludes with the same, after reversing the order of words in the second half of the line, thus illustrating how the one who spills blood will have the situation reversed on him and at last have his own blood spilled. Uses of this figure of sound are also found in Proverbs.

Texts

Proverbs 10.26. In this proverbial simile the two images are indicated

1. This and the following example are described in A. Strus, 'La poétique sonore des récits de la Genèse', *Bib* 60 (1979), p. 16; also (independently) in J.S. Kselman, 'Semantic-Sonant Chiasmus in Biblical Poetry', *Bib* 58 (1977), p. 220.

by the same sequence and these in turn are echoed by the same sounds in the second colon.

a.	*kaḥōmeṣ laššinnayim*	Like vinegar to the teeth and like smoke to
	wᵉke'āšān lā'ênāyim	the eyes,
b.	*kēn he'āṣēl lᵉšōleḥāyw*	so the lazy man to the one who sends him.

In the first colon the two images of vinegar and smoke share a sequence of the same sounds, /k, (ṣ, š), l, n/.

a. *kḥmṣ lšnayim* *wk'šn l'ynāyim*
k ṣ lšnayim *k šn l nāyim*

The dual endings on the second word of each simile help both to distinguish each half of that colon and also to link them together. Thus, the sound patterns follow the syntax of the colon and serve to emphasize or mark it. Each simile, in other words, echoes or repeats the major sounds of the other and in almost the same sequence.

When the second colon is considered, that to which the similes are compared, the pattern is the same.

b. *kn h'ṣl lšlḥyw*
kn ṣl lšl

The /k/ leads off again and is followed mainly by a sound pattern using /l/ and sibilants. Thus, the third part of the simile is 'tagged'. But this colon also echoes other sounds in the first colon. The initial /l, š/ motif of *lšnym* of the first simile is repeated in *lšlḥyw*. The /', ā, (š, ṣ)/ motif of *ke'āšān* from the second simile is echoed in the word *hᵉ'āṣēl*.[1]

a. *kḥmṣ lšnym wᵉke'āšān l'ynym* b. *kn he'āṣēl lšlḥyw*
lš *'āš* *'āṣ lš*

Each image from the first colon finds an echo in the second colon.

Proverbs 11.10. A sequence of consonants in the first colon marks off some of the grammatical units therein.

a.	*bᵉṭûb ṣaddîqîm ta'ᵃlōṣ qiryâ*	In the prosperity of the just the city rejoices,
b.	*ûba'ᵃbōd rᵉšā'îm rinnâ*	and when the wicked perish there is jubilation.

The consonantal motif of the first colon is /(ṭ, t), ṣ, q/:

1. Boström, *Paronomasi*, p. 126.

a. *bṭwb ṣdyqym* *t'lṣ qryh*
ṭ ṣ q *t ṣ q*

The prepositional phrase *bṭwb ṣdyqym*, used as the verbal object, is thus distinguished from and yet tied to the next unit in the colon, the verb and its subject, *t'lṣ qryh*. The second colon does not have this type of sound pattern. Instead, each half of the second colon echoes sounds of the same half of the first colon. The first halves have a matching alliterative sequence of sounds:

a. *bṭwb ṣdyqîm . . .* b. *wb'bd rš'îm . . .*
b b d îm *b bd îm*

These sound patterns closely associate the two main contrasting themes of the proverb, the prosperity of the just and the destruction of the wicked. The remaining halves of the two cola round off this euphony with other sounds, including end rhyme:

a. *. . . qiryâ* b. *. . . rinnâ*
ir â *ri â*

This rhyme indirectly suggests by sound the synonymous conclusions of both cola: with either the success of the just or the failure of the wicked the result is the same—the city rejoices.

Proverbs 16.23. Tagging sound patterns appear in each colon of this proverb.

a. *lēb ḥākām yaśkîl pîhû* The wise-hearted one makes his mouth prudent,
b. *w^e'al ś^epātāyw yōsîp leqaḥ* and adds persuasiveness to his lips.

The pattern in the first colon is /l, (b, p), k/. In the second colon it is /l, (ś, s), p/. Note the chiasmus created in each case:

a. *lb ḥkm* *yśkyl pyhw*
lb k *k l p*

b. *w'l śptyw* *ysyp lqḥ*
l śp *s p l*

What is interesting about these particular patterns and what makes them noticeable is that the second half of each colon echoes the first half. In the first colon the subject, *lb ḥkm*, is echoed by the predicate, *yśkyl pyhw*; in the second colon the predicate, *ysyp lqḥ*, echoes the prepositional phrase, *w'l śptyw*.

Definite grammatical units in the colon, consequently, are tagged and bound together by sounds. When the consonant /ś/ of the predicate in the first colon is considered along with the sounds /l/ and /p/ therein, this phrase is itself tied by consonance to the two grammatical units of the second colon:

a.	*. . . yśkyl pyhw*	b.	*w'l śptyw ysyp lqḥ*
	ś l p		*l śp s p l*

A /y, (ś, s), î, p/ alliteration between the two predicates furthers the ties between the cola. This, plus the fact that the subject of the first colon has a clear link by consonance with the final word of the proverb, creates another chiasmus.

a.	*lēb ḥākām yaśkîl pîhû*	b.	*w^e'al ś^epātāyw yōsîp leqaḥ*
	l ḥ k y ś î p		*y sîp l q ḥ*

The whole thrust of this sound pattern seems to be toward the final phrase, *ysyp lqḥ*, which contains all the dominant sounds of the proverb in itself. The addition of persuasiveness is the crown to the person's wisdom and prudence.

A third chiasmus of the semantic-sonant type[1] binds the whole proverb. The semantic half of the chiasmus is formed by the parallel pair *pyhw* and *śptyw*, while the /l, ḥ, (k, q)/ consonance already mentioned forms the sonant half.

a.	*lb ḥkm yśkyl pyhw*	b.	*w'l śptyw ysyp lqḥ*
	l ḥk pyhw		*śptyw lqḥ*

All in all, chiasmus operates on every level in this proverb. It is found within each colon, then between the cola, joining them with two different patterns. Each chiasmus underlines a particular aspect of the proverb.

Proverbs 19.28. The sounds of *bly'l* and *ybl'* become the major tagging sounds of this proverb.

a.	*'ēd b^eliyya'al yālîṣ mišpāṭ*	A worthless witness mocks justice
b.	*ûpî r^ešā'îm y^eballa' 'āwen*	and the mouth of the wicked (avidly) devours trouble.

In the first colon the labials /b, p/, the dentals /d, ṭ/, plus /y/ and /l/,

1. Kselman, 'Semantic-Sonant Chiasmus', pp. 219-20.

form a chiastic sequence that is evenly divided between subject and predicate.

a. *'d bly'l* *ylyṣ mšpṭ*
d bly l *yl pṭ*
ṣ š

An additional consonance of sibilants reinforces the bond between verb, *ylyṣ*, and object, *mšpṭ*. The phonic sequence of the second colon is less dramatic, /(p, b), '/, and is chiastically reversed in the second half of the colon.

b. *wpy rš'ym* *ybl' 'wn*
p ' *b '*

Again the pattern divides evenly between subject and predicate.

Some critics, uneasy with the idea of the wicked 'swallowing' evil, prefer to read in the second colon *yabbîa'*, 'spew forth', as in Prov. 15.28, instead of the MT *y*^{e}*balla'*.[1] Boström comments:

> But, first of all, *ybl'* is an unmistakable allusion to *bly'l*, which the Frankenberg-Toy proposal of *yby'* overlooks. The LXX also has καταπίεται.[2]

In support of *y*^{e}*balla'* Delitzsch suggests the comparable image in Job 15.16b:[3]

'îš šōteh kammayim 'awlâ a man who drinks iniquity like water

There is also the longer passage in the same book, 20.12-15, where the punishment of the wicked is described in terms of food (his wickedness) which will turn sour in the stomach (his wickedness will turn against him). In the case of this proverb, 'devouring trouble' means that wickedness 'is a delicious morsel for the mouth of the godless, which he eagerly devours; to practice evil is for him, as we

1. *BHS*; Toy, *A Critical Commentary*, pp. 381-82; Scott, *Proverbs*, p. 117; Gemser, *Sprüche*, p. 77; and Ringgren, *Sprüche*, p. 78. *HALAT* (p. 129) views this verb as from a distinct root, *bl'* II, which means 'communicate, inform'. For another view, see N.J. Tromp, *Primitive Conceptions of Death and the Nether World in the Old Testament* (BibOr, 21; Rome: Pontifical Biblical Institute, 1969), pp. 125-28.

2. Boström, *Paronomasi*, p. 178.

3. Delitzsch, *Biblical Commentary*, VI.2, p. 38.

say, "ein wahrer Genuss". . .'[1] The sound patterning of the proverb would also tend to confirm the MT. As Boström indicated above, there is consonance between *bly'l*, 'the worthless one', of the first colon and the verb *ybl'*, 'devours', of the second colon, which would support the notion of an intentional wordplay. The difficulty with 'swallowing' evil could be removed by viewing it as oxymoron: the false witness mocks justice by bringing forth words from his mouth, but by acting in this way he is really swallowing evil. In addition, the phonic correlation between *bly'l* and *ybl'* brings *bly'l* into association with the *rš'ym* and highlights the fact that *'d bly'l* and *py rš'ym* are synonymous. Although none of these arguments are in themselves absolutely conclusive, it does seem clear the MT *ybl'* is correct, however it is to be interpreted. This once again indicates the need for considering sound patterns seriously when questioning even the wording of a particular text.

Proverbs 17.25. In this proverb are two predicates, one in each colon, surrounding *bēn k^esîl*, the subject in the first colon.

a.	*ka'as l^e'ābîw bēn k^esîl*	A provocation to his father is a foolish son
b.	*ûmemer l^eyôladtô*	and bitterness for the one who bore him.

Another way of expressing this pattern is to say that the subject, though shared in sense by both cola, is expressed only once. The proverb can be diagrammed as follows:

a.	*k's*	*l'byw*	*bn ksyl*
	A	B	C
b.	*wmmr*	*lywldtw*	
	A′	B′	

Although the pattern ties the two predicates together, the sound patterning goes in another direction and associates the subject with the predicate of the first colon. The sequence of sounds clearly distinguishes these two elements of the grammatical structure.

a.	*k's l'byw*	*bn ksyl*
	k s l b	*b ks l*

What is being said about the son (the predicate) is echoed in the son's full name, *bn ksyl*. The only phonic pattern in the second colon is the

1. Delitzsch, *Biblical Commentary*, VI.2, p. 38.

repetition of /l, ô/ in the one word *l^e^yôladtô*. The double /l/ here picks up the double /l/ in the first colon.

The second colon is noticeably short and it has often been suggested that something has dropped out after *lywldtw*. The limited sound patterning of the colon as contrasted with the first colon may support this view, although the syllable count in each colon is nearly the same (7, 7).

In summary, accepting the MT as it stands, the sense parallelism emphasizes the relationship between the cola, while the sound patterning keeps the cola distinct as if thereby to draw attention to the different people affected by *bn ksyl* and the distinct ways in which he affects them.

Proverbs 19.26. A deliberate choice of words here is underscored by the intercola consonance. This same consonance also indicates the various grammatical units of the proverb.

a.	*m^e^šadded 'āb yabrîaḥ 'ēm*	He who mistreats father, who drives mother away,
b.	*bēn mēbîš ûmaḥpîr*	is a shameful and disgraceful son.

This proverb, the subject of which is the first colon and predicate the second colon, relates various words in a way that might be described as 'fitting the punishment to the crime'. The *bēn mēbîš* of the second colon is associated by a consonantal motif /m, b, š/ with *m^e^šadded 'āb*, his first-mentioned crime, thus also marking off the first phrase in the subject colon and tying it to the first half of the predicate:

a.	*mšdd 'b ybryḥ 'm*	b.	*bn mbyš wmḥpyr*
	mš b		*b mb š*

The phrase *ybrḥ 'm*, the second half of the subject colon, which refers to the son's second crime, is related to *maḥpîr*, the second epithet for *bēn* and the latter half of the predicate, by another motif /m, ḥ, (p, b), r/.[1]

a.	*mšdd 'b ybryḥ 'm*	b.	*bn mbyš wmḥpyr*
	br ḥ m		*mḥp r*

In this latter relationship there is also the long /i/ assonance in *yabrîaḥ* and *maḥpîr*. These sound patterns very definitely challenge the argu-

1. Boström, *Paronomasi*, pp. 177-78.

ments of those who wish to change *mšdd* to *mndd* on lexicographical grounds alone.[1]

Proverbs 15.8. In the next proverb intercola sound patterning delineates all parts of the antithetic parallelism.

a.	*zebaḥ rᵉšā'îm tô'ᵃbat* YHWH	The sacrifice of the wicked is abhorrent to the Lord,
b.	*ûtᵉpillat yᵉšārîm rᵉṣônô*	but the prayer of the just is his delight.

This is one of several sayings in Proverbs that refer to cult and sacrifice. Although *zebaḥ* and *tᵉpillâ* would usually be, in the broad sense, synonymous, their particular context in this saying makes them antithetic. By associating 'the wicked' with 'sacrifice', the proverb has turned *zebaḥ* into something abhorrent.[2]

The use of *rᵉšā'îm* and *yᵉšārîm* is significant also for the resulting sounds. The alliteration found in those words establishes a bond between the cola which broadens with the use of other sounds into a pattern including both cola entirely. First of all, there are various phonic links from word to word, phrase to phrase and, thence, from colon to colon.

a. *zbḥ rš'ym tw'bt* YHWH	b. *wtplt yšrym rṣwnw*
b ' 'b	
z rš	*šr rṣ*
t bt y	*tp t y*

Since the final link (*šr* and *rṣ*) echoes sounds at the very beginning of the proverb (*z* and *rš*) and another pattern, /t, (b, p), t, y/, binds the end of the first colon with the beginning of the second, a sound pattern marks each half of the proverb creating, as a result, a chiastic phonic motif for the whole proverb.

a. *zbḥ rᵉšā'îm tw'bt* YHWH	b. *wtplt yᵉšārîm rṣwnw*
z rᵉšā îm t bt y	*tp t yᵉšārîm rṣ*

1. Toy, *A Critical Commentary*, p. 382; D.W. Thomas ('Some Passages in the Book of Proverbs', in *Wisdom in Israel and in the Ancient Near East* [ed. M. Noth and D.W. Thomas; VTSup, 3; Leiden: Brill, 1960], p. 289) proposes, for the sake of clearer synonymity with *yabrîaḥ*, translating *mšdd* as 'expel, eject' on the basis of Ethiopic *sadada*; and, similarly, see van der Weiden, *Le livre*, p. 131.

2. See the discussion in L.G. Perdue, *Wisdom and Cult* (SBLDS, 30; Missoula, MT: Scholars Press, 1977), pp. 155-58.

Proverbs 22.13. Besides its tagging sound pattern, this proverb is also a good example of caricature, and the use of exaggeration and irony as an effective mode of expression.

a.	*'āmar 'āṣēl 'ᵃrî baḥûṣ*	The lazy one cries: 'A lion's outside!
b.	*bᵉtôk rᵉḥōbôt 'ērāṣēaḥ*	I could be killed in the middle of the streets!'

The proverb is a classic case of ironic hyperbole; the lazy person gives a wild and silly excuse for his behavior.[1] The tagging sound pattern leads in an unmistakeable way up to the final, outlandish remark. The pattern involves the sequence /r, ṣ/, which occurs twice in the first colon, distinguishing the opening introduction from the direct quotation:

a. *'mr 'ṣl 'ry bḥwṣ*
r ṣ r ṣ

The same sequence appears again only in the last word of the saying, *'ērāṣēaḥ*. Thus, the excuse receives emphasis from the sounds of the words themselves.

If one looks at the cola separately, sound patterns which distinguish them can be seen. The first colon has the sequence /r, ṣ/, which has already been illustrated. The second colon has a twice-repeated pattern of /b, t, r, ḥ/:

b. *btwk rḥbwt 'rṣḥ*
bt rḥb t r ḥ

The repetition and overlapping of these sounds in such a straightforward and simple manner may be meant to turn the speech of the *'āṣēl* into bombastic doggerel—the foolish *'āṣēl* says silly things in a silly way. In Isa. 28.10 and 13 just such exaggerated repetition is used to mock Isaiah's speech:

ṣaw lāṣāw ṣaw lāṣāw
qaw lāqāw qaw lāqāw
zᵉ'êr šām zᵉ'êr šām

But the sounds in the proverb are not as pronounced as in Isaiah.

Proverbs 26.13. It is interesting to compare Prov. 22.13 with its near twin 26.13.

1. McKane, *Proverbs*, p. 569; Gemser, *Sprüche*, p. 83.

a. *'āmar 'āṣēl šaḥal baddārek* The lazy one cries: 'A lion's on the road!
b. *'ᵃrî bên hārᵉḥōbôt* A lion's within the street!'

The sound patterning is less dramatic in this version. The first colon has a pattern /r, (ṣ, š), l/ which again distinguishes the two halves of that colon. The second colon has a /r, b/ sequence.

a. *'mr 'ṣl šḥl bdrk*
r ṣl š l r

b. *'ry byn hrḥbwt*
r b r b

This proverb achieves its ironic and exaggerated tone simply by repeating the silly cry of the *'āṣēl*. The sound patterns relate the various parts of the proverb one to another but less dramatically.

Proverbs 29.10. There is a major problem with meaning in the second colon of this proverb. The MT has the following:

a. *'anšê dāmîm yiśnᵉ'û tām*
b. *wîšārîm yᵉbaqqᵉšû napšô*

The normal meaning of the words would require this translation:

a. Bloodthirsty men hate the honest person,
b. and the upright seek his life.

This is unacceptable for obvious reasons. The problem centers around the phrase *ybqšw npšw* in the second colon, which is common, idiomatic Hebrew for 'to try to kill (someone)'. But such an attribution to the 'upright' is impossible.

To solve the problem, the word *wyšrym* in the second colon could be changed to *wrš'ym* and the results would give a proverb with synonymous parallelism:

Bloodthirsty men hate the honest person,
and the *wicked* seek his life.[1]

Another solution is to substitute the verb *bqr* for *bqš*, with the sense of 'having care for, being concerned about'.[2] This change would yield an antithetic meaning in the second colon:

. . . but the upright *are concerned for* his life.

1. *BHS* suggests this change.
2. *BHS*; Scott, *Proverbs*, p. 168 n. f; Gemser, *Sprüche*, p. 101.

Others have tried to deal with the text as it is without changing it. Delitzsch places the pause after *wîšārîm* and then renders the whole saying:

a. Men of blood hate the guiltless
b. and the upright; they attempt the life of such[1]

But such a division of the lines goes against the very typical parallelism and symmetry of the cola in the sayings throughout Proverbs.[2] Another suggestion is to understand *bqš* in the sense of 'revenge' or 'demand an accounting for' (which is probably the understanding of the LXX, which uses the verb ἐκζητέω, 'search eagerly for, avenge'). But this is not in keeping with the general attitude of Proverbs, which never attributes such judicial roles to the *yšrym*.[3] Can a study of sound patterning in the proverb contribute to a solution?

An examination of the sounds of the proverb shows clearly that *bqš* belongs. First of all, there is strong sibilant consonance linking the whole saying, particularly the second colon, which would be weakened by the use of *bqr* instead of *bqš*.

a. *'nšy dmym yśn'w tm* b. *wyšrym ybqšw npšw*
š *ś* *š* *š* *š*

In the first colon a tagging sound pattern, /n, (š, ś, (d, t), am/, distinguishes subject and predicate. Furthermore, consonants of *'nšy* are echoed in the opposite order in the verb *yśn'w*, and *dmym* is echoed in the word *tm*. There is even alliteration between the words *dām* and *tām*.[4]

a. *'nšy dāmym yśn'w tām*
nš dām śn tām

Linking sound patterns join the first and second cola. The /(š, ś), n/ combination of *'nšy* and *yśn'w* is found also in *npšw*. This brings the hate (*yśn'w*) of the bloodthirsty men (*'nšy*) into direct conflict with the honest person's life (*npšw*), a conflict brought about completely

1. Delitzsch, *Biblical Commentary*, VI.2, pp. 246-47.
2. Toy (*A Critical Commentary*, p. 509) calls such a revision 'an unsymmetrical division of lines and a loose grammatical form'.
3. Delitzsch, *Biblical Commentary*, VI.2, p. 247.
4. Boström, *Paronomasi*, p. 112.

by sound. On the other hand, the verb in the second colon, *ybqšw*, is also associated with *npšw* by the /(b, p), š / motif in each.

a. *'nšy dmym yśn'w tm* b. *wyšrym ybqšw npšw*
nš *śn* *n š*
b š *pš*

Overall, the sound patterning of the proverb gives a strong indication that the *ybqšw* should remain despite the problem it causes.

If the MT is to be accepted as it is, then, and the phrase *bqš npš* retains its usual meaning of 'seek to kill', the word *wyšrym* has to be changed to *wrš'ym* to make any sense. This would not break up any sound patterns in the proverb. The solution amounts to keeping the MT where a change would interrupt sound patterns (*bqš*) and emending the text where the phonic structure would not be affected (*wyšrym* to *wrš'ym*).

On the other hand, the LXX reading εὐθεῖς would seem to support MT *wyšrym*. Is there any way the full MT text (with both *wyšrym* and *bqš*) can be upheld? Boström suggests interpreting the phrase *ybqšw npšw* as a pun.[1] The presence of *wyšrym* in the second colon completely reverses the meaning of the phrase from 'seeking to kill life' to 'seeking to preserve life'. By alluding to the *'nšy dmym* in its proper sense and characterizing the *yšrym* in its new, reversed meaning, the word *bqš* was meant to focus the complete dichotomy of views between the two personalities being described. However, there are few passages in the OT to support such an interpretation of *bqš npš*.[2] The phrase *l^ebaqqēš 'al napšô* in Esth. 7.7, which describes Haman as 'begging for his life', is close, but the presence of the preposition *'al* in the Esther passage qualifies the similarity. That *bqš* itself is used for seeking good is verified by Ps. 122.9b, Neh. 2.10 and Eccl. 3.15,[3] but these too are not adequate for verifying Boström's proposal. Appeal can be had to comparable examples in English where the context has completely changed the meaning of words. The words 'grave man', for instance, always mean 'serious man' except when on

1. Boström, *Paronomasi*, p. 113.
2. Several commentators feel constrained to give *bqš npš* a positive translation despite its usual meaning. Gemser (*Sprüche*, p. 114) renders it 'to have a high regard for'; Barucq (*Le livre*, p. 214) translates it as 'seek out his company' by comparing the Proverbs phrase to *bqš pnym*.
3. Examples are from Zorell, *Lexicon*, p. 125.

the lips of the dying Mercutio, in Shakespeare's *Romeo and Juliet*: 'Ask for me tomorrow and you shall find me a grave man'.[1] Perhaps the 'undoing' of the normal sense of *bqš* is meant to suggest that the good man can 'undo' the machinations of the wicked.

There the problem must remain. An analysis of the proverb's sound patterns will not give a definitive interpretation. Nonetheless, it helps to indicate limits within which a legitimate answer should be sought and forestalls hasty corrections of the text which may well impair the poetic structure or meaning.

1. Example appears under 'Pun' in *Dictionary of World Literary Terms* (ed. J.T. Shipley; Boston: The Writer, rev. edn, 1970), p. 260.

Chapter 6

TAGGING SOUND PATTERNS (2)

1. *Coordinating Proverbs*

Introduction

There is a type of proverb that attracts tagging sound patterns in a more striking manner than those already described. This type achieves conciseness of expression by the simple coordination of images, persons, things or ideas and the omission of other words, which, though required for the syntax, are not required for understanding. The ellipsis of these words renders the proverb ambivalent and suggestive, but also compact and succinct, amply fulfilling Scott's definition of a proverb as

> . . . a short, pregnant sentence or phrase whose meaning is applicable in many situations, with imagery or striking verbal form to assist the memory. It has been well described as having shortness, sense and salt.[1]

For example, there is the English proverb 'Grasp all, lose all'. It is crisp and compact, shorn of all but the most necessary words to make sense. But the precise syntactical construction of the proverb remains ambivalent. It could be an imperative followed by an elliptical apodosis ('Grasp all, then you will lose all') or an elliptical condition ('If you were to grasp all, then you would lose all'). But neither of these full syntactical constructions is proverbial. They have not reduced the truth to its most compact and expressive form. They less effectively highlight the relationship between 'grasping' and 'losing' (oxymoron) than does the form of the proverb with the simple coordination of the two phrases. In fact, the very attractiveness and aesthetic appeal of this form of expression seems to wane the more

1. R.B.Y. Scott, *The Way of Wisdom in the Old Testament* (New York: Macmillan, 1971), p. 58.

complex it becomes. Thus, a fuller elaboration of the same proverb leaves the idea bare and unappealing:

> If you try to get everything in life,
> you'll never be able to hold onto anything!

In addition, its form is too long to be remembered with ease.

The sound patterns associated with these proverbs often underscore the coordination of terms with matching or similar phonic motifs in both parts of the coordination. Thus, in 'Grasp all, lose all' the similar sibilant sounds and the repetition of 'all' in both halves of the proverb occur in the same order, creating an appealing and symmetrical phonic structure which emphasizes the coordination.

Grasp all,	lose all
s all	s all

The ear as well as the sense draws the mind's attention to the relationship being established between these seemingly contradictory notions. No further syntactical structure or expanded description is necessary for the meaning.

In the saying, 'Much light, much shadow', the use of 'light' and 'shadow' is striking because those terms are ordinarily antithetic: 'light' is the negation of 'shadow' and 'shadow' is the absence or obstruction of 'light'. The sound pattern involving the repetition of 'much' at the beginning of each half of the proverb highlights the connection being made. Thus, the sound pattern, as well as the oxymoron of the proverb, points to a truth underlying the apparent contradictions: without light there is no shadow; and the more light there is, the sharper and deeper the shadow. The tagging sound patterning in this type of proverb marks the coordination of terms or ideas. The use of the same sounds on both sides of the coordination, often in the exact same order, 'portrays' the relationship for the ear.

The proverb need not be composed of apparent contradictions. A logical sequence of ideas is behind the proverb, 'Out of sight, out of mind'. But the force of that logic is brought home very sharply by the repetition of the prepositional phrase 'out of', which both emphasizes the coordination of ideas and also points to what is being related ('sight' and 'mind'). The connection between the ideas in 'Nothing ventured, nothing gained' is reinforced by the word repetition, the end rhyme in /ed/ of both participles, and by the repeating /n/:

Nothing ventured,	nothing gained.
nothing n ed	nothing ned

This particular type of tagging sound pattern helps make the coordinating proverb a very emphatic statement.

Texts

Proverbs 12.5. Coordination is found in both cola of this proverb.

a.	*maḥšᵉbôt ṣaddîqîm mišpāṭ*	The plans of the just are sound judgment;
b.	*taḥbūlôt rᵉšāʿîm mirmâ*	the counsels of the wicked are treachery.

The nominal sentence structures in this proverb simply join *mḥšbwt* and *mšpṭ* in the first colon, then *tḥblwt* and *mrmh* in the second. Thus, this proverb says about the just's plans, for instance, what Prov. 20.18 says with the verb *tkwn* ('succeed'), or what Prov. 21.5 says with the phrase *'k lmwtr* ('only to plenty'). It merely joins *mḥšbwt ṣdyqym* with *mšpṭ* grammatically to convey the same general idea. The word *mšpṭ* is customarily used of legal decisions or judgments that have some binding force. What the just plan, therefore, or what their plans produce, is given the status of such decisions by the simple coordination of words: 'the plans of the just—*mišpāṭ*!' The word *mrmh* refers to anything that is opposed to *mšpṭ*—cheating (Amos 8.5; Prov. 11.1), treason (2 Kgs 9.23), false witnessing and lying (Prov. 12.17; Isa. 53.9), especially the latter. Thus, the counsels of the wicked and what it leads to are condemned. The perfect grammatical and antithetic parallelism broadens the meaning of these six words further.

a.	*mḥšbwt*	*ṣdyqym*	*mšpṭ*
	A	B	C
b.	*tḥblwt*	*ršʿym*	*mrmh*
	A′	B′	C′

The contrast implies that 'the plans of the just' are never 'treacherous', and that 'the wicked's plans' can never be described as 'sound' or 'just'. Small and compact though it is, the proverb is rich in meaning. In fact, the very compactness lends itself better to suggestion and implication than a wordy, precise and clearly defined statement.

Enhancing the coordinations are the sound patterns. In the first colon sounds from the two main words (*mḥšbwt* and *mšpṭ*) mark off the coordination:

a. *mḥšbwt ṣdyqym mšpṭ*
m šb t mšpṭ

The sound pattern leads right to *mšpṭ*. In the second colon the pattern is less striking but nonetheless present in the second and third words. It is, basically, the consonants of the final word as they are echoed in the preceding phrase.

b. *tḥblwt rš'ym mrmh*
r m mrm

In addition, intercola sound patterns in the proverb mark off the semantic antitheses in chiastic fashion as follows:

a. *maḥšᵉbôt ṣaddîqîm mišpāṭ* b. *taḥbūlôt rᵉšā'îm mirmâ*
ḥ bôt ṣ îm mi *ḥb ôt š 'îm mi*

The proverb produces interrelated patterns of sound, grammar, and sense.

Participles are a common means of creating coordination in nominal sentences in the Hebrew proverbs as the next example and the many after it will amply illustrate.

Proverbs 20.19. This proverb has two tagging sound patterns, the one in the first colon marking the coordination of two participial phrases.

a. *gôleh sôd hôlēk rākîl* One who reveals secrets is a tale-bearer;
b. *ûlᵉpōteh śᵉpātāyw lō' tit'ārāb* so have nothing to do with a babbler!

First of all, the /o/ assonance, especially the long /o/ plus /e/ vowels of the participles, draws the whole proverb together. Another sound pattern involves the alliteration of /ol/, which appears in *gôleh* and *hôlēk* and is echoed in *lᵉpōteh* and *lō'* of the second colon. The final *lō'* is particularly highlighted by this latter pattern.

a. *gôleh sôd hôlēk rākîl* b. *ûlᵉpōteh śᵉpātāyw lō' tit'ārāb*
ô e ô ô ē *ō e ō*
ôl ôl *l ō lō*

Secondly, each colon has its own distinctive set of sounds. The phrase *gôleh sôd*, in the first colon, has a /g, l/ sequence that is echoed in the /l, k/ pattern of *hôlēk rākîl*, the phrase which follows where the sequences /l, k/ and /k, l/ are chiastic. Thus, the grammatical coordination of 'tale-bearer' and 'revealer of secrets' is echoed as well by the sounds of the proverb. In the second colon the participial phrase *pōteh śᵉpātāyw* has a /p, t/ motif which, with the preceding /l/, is echoed in the /l, t, t, b/ sequence of the last phrase of the proverb, *lō' tit'ārāb*. Thus, the sound pattern in the second colon distinguishes the command, *lō' tit'ārāb*, from its object, *lpth śptyw*. The full patterning of the proverb appears like this:

a.	*gwlh swd*	*hwlk rkyl*
	g l	*lk k l*
b.	*wlpth śptyw*	*l'tt'rb*
	lpt pt	*l tt b*

The pronounced labial motif of the second colon may be an attempt to mimic the 'babbler', which word itself is probably of onomatopoeic origin.

It is interesting to note how *l' tt'rb* at the end of the second colon is different from the rest of the proverb. The three preceding participles set up a pattern, both grammatical and phonic, which is broken by this final verb phrase. This type of construction in the proverbs, where a pattern of participles or participial phrases is concluded by a non-participial word or phrase, may well be intended as a signal of the end of the proverb. The change in the pattern alerts the hearer to the remark that concludes the proverb. The same type of construction will be noted in some of the proverbs which follow.

Proverbs 11.13. An interesting comparison can be made between this proverb and the one just studied, 20.19.

a.	*hôlēk rākîl mᵉgalleh sôd*	A tale-bearer is one who reveals secrets,
b.	*wᵉneʼᵉman rûaḥ mᵉkasseh dābār*	but a trustworthy person is one who keeps a matter confidential.

The first colon of each saying is nearly identical; but there is little /o/ assonance in this proverb. This first colon follows the same sound pattern as in Prov. 20.19a, only in reverse. The second colon of 11.13 is a perfect antithesis to the first and loses completely the /p, b/ motif present in 20.19b, which added to the sound effects there. The second colon here has a /m, r/ sequence.

a. *hwlk rkyl* *mglh swd*
lk k l *gl*
b. *wn'mn rwḥ* *mksh dbr*
m r *m r*

The connection between the two cola is forged by grammatical and semantic parallelism as well as by sound:

a. *hwlk rkyl* *mglh swd*
A B
b. *wn'mn rwḥ* *mksh dbr*
A′ B′

The two antagonistic personalities (A and A′) are precise opposites. They share the sound of /a/ vowels (*ne'eman* and *rākîl*) and the consonant /r/ in *rākî* and *rûaḥ*. The predicates also represent opposite types of people (B and B′) but share more sound patterning than the subjects. First of all, both begin with the identical alliterative pattern of a *piel* participle, /mĕ + consonant + a + doubled consonant + eh/: *megalleh* and *mekasseh*. The *piel* form for *glh* is used here and not the *qal* form as in 20.19a because of the different sound patterns in each proverb. With *glh*, the *qal* and *piel* forms mean practically the same thing, 'uncover', but the *qal* form in 20.19a corresponds to the other *qal* participles in that proverb: *hôlēk* and *pōteh*.[1] In 11.13a the *piel* form was used in order to match *mekasseh*,[2] which is almost exclusively used in the *piel*.[3] Secondly, both predicates share the

1. E. Jenni (*Das hebräische Pi'el* [Zürich: EVZ-Verlag, 1968], p. 203) attempts to distinguish slight differences in the sense of the *qal* and *piel* here, but this seems artificial. Even if he is correct, it is still clear that the *sense* of neither proverb is seriously changed by switching the participles. In both cases sound was the prime determinant in the choice of form.

2. Joüon (*Grammaire*, §51.b) illustrates a similar matching of forms: the *niphal* infinitive absolute has two forms—the most frequent *hiqqāṭēl* form is used with the imperfect verbal form *yiqqāṭēl*; the other form *niqṭōl* is used with the *niphal* perfect *niqṭal*.

3. In the active sense *ksh* is almost always *piel*. There are only three cases of *ksh* in the *qal* (*HALAT*, p. 464). Two cases, Prov. 12.16 and 23, are surely for reasons of sound (for Prov. 12.16, see Chapter 7). The third usage is the *qal* passive participle (*kesûy*) in Ps. 32.1, where sound patterning clearly explains both participles there:

'šry neśûy (from *nś'*) *pš'*
kesûy ḥṭ'h

sounds of the sequence /m, (g, k), s, d/:

a.	. . . *m^egalleh sôd*	b.	. . . *m^ekasseh dābār*
	m^ega eh		*m^eka eh*
	m g s d		*m k ss d*

Proverbs 15.32. The following proverb is made up of four participial phrases.

a.	*pôrēa' mûsār mô'ēs napšô*	One who ignores discipline is one who rejects his own self,
b.	*w^ešômēa' tôkaḥat qôneh lēb*	but one attentive to correction is one who gains understanding.

The coordination in this saying involves oxymoron: the one who avoids discipline is not saving himself from anything but is actually destroying himself, while being harsh on oneself really does not subvert the self but leads to enlightenment. The force of these apparent contradictions is emphasized by the contrast with their 'antitheses' in the opposite colon: 'one who ignores discipline' is not 'one who gains understanding', nor will the one who accepts discipline ever risk 'rejecting his own self'. These complex relationships are starkly defined by the four participial phrases.

Sound patterns also help define the coordinated units in this proverb. Most of all, the participial vowel pattern of a long /o/ followed by /e/ is a strong, obvious assonance in the proverb which marks the first word of each half of the coordination in both cola.

a.	*pôrēa' mûsār*	*mô'ēs napšô*
	ô ē	*ô ē*
b.	*w^ešômēa' tôkaḥat*	*qôneh lēb*
	ô ē	*ô e*

Besides assonance there is consonance. The two halves of the first colon are brought together by other sounds as well:[1]

a.	*pwr' mwsr*	*mw's npšw*
	p m s	*m s pš*

The syllable /šô/ creates a bond between *napšô*, at the end of the first colon, and *šômēa'*, the first word of the second colon. An alliterative sound pattern reflecting the coordination in the second colon is to be found in the sounds of /ôk/ and /qô/ in *twkḥt* and *qwnh*.

1. Boström, *Paronomasi*, p. 156.

b. *wšwm' tôkaḥat qôneh lb*
ôk qô

Finally, there is alliteration based on the motif /ô, ē, '/ found in the initial words of both cola: *pôrēa'* and *šômēa'*.[1] The grammatical symmetry of this proverb is thus highlighted by the phonic symmetry.

Proverbs 13.3. This proverb contains three participial phrases.

a.	*nōṣēr pîw šōmēr napšô*	One who watches his mouth is one who guards his life;
b.	*pōśēq śᵉpātāyw mᵉḥittâ lô*	one who opens his lips wide—destruction is for him!

The coordination of participial phrases in the first colon is used to characterize different types of people who belong together. After *pōśēq*, however, the second colon does not continue the participial format but concludes with the phrase *mᵉḥittâ lô*, also used in Prov. 18.7 and similar to the phrase in 10.14b. The use of this phrase creates a break in the sequence of participles and draws attention to the concluding remark of the proverb.[2] The juxtaposition of phrases in the second colon is also an indication of the flexible and suggestive combinations of words which are possible. The Hebrew is saying in as succinct and striking a way as possible: 'the babbler and destruction go hand in hand!'

Even more arresting is the sound patterning in this proverb. The participles *nōṣēr* and *šōmēr* are an alliterative pair of roots that appear frequently as parallels in Hebrew poetry.[3] The /(n, m), (ṣ, š), r/ pattern that links these words is also picked up at the end of the first colon by *napšô*, which continues the nasal and sibilant sounds and uses /p/ to form a bond with *pîw*. The result is a pattern of the same sounds, which distinguishes and matches both halves of the first colon:

a. *nṣr pyw šmr npšw*
nṣr p šmr npš

In addition there is the repetition of the long /o/ vowel throughout the colon, and the repetition of the long /o/ plus /e/ participial vowel

1. Boström, *Paronomasi*, p. 156.
2. See Prov. 20.19, Chapter 6.
3. A. Fitzgerald, 'A Note on G-Stem *YNṢR* Forms in the Old Testament', *ZAW* 84 (1972), p. 91.

pattern in *nōṣēr* and *šōmēr* to mark off the beginning of each half of the colon. Then, the /p/ and sibilants are brought from the first colon of the proverb to the second by *pōśēq śᵉpātāyw*, the first two words in the second colon.[1] The other repeating sounds in that colon are /t/ in *śptyw* and *mḥth* and the sound of long /o/ linking the first and last words, thus:

b.	*pōśq*	*śptyw*	*mḥth*	*lô*
	p ś	*śp*		
	ō	*t*	*t*	*ô*

Furthermore, the last word of the first colon, *napšô*, is echoed by *pōśēq* at the beginning of the second, with the repetition of the sequence /p, (š, ś), o/. And there is assonance at the end of both cola with the /o/ vowel of *napšô* and *lô*.

a.	. . . *napšô*	b.	*pōśēq* . . .	*lô*
	pšô		*pōś*	*ô*

The following diagram shows the grammatical parallelism of the proverb:

a.	*nṣr*		*pyw*		*šmr*		*npšw*
	part.	+	gen.	+	part.	+	gen.
		subj.		+		pred.	
b.	*pśq*		*śptyw*		*mḥth*		lw
	part.	+	gen.	+	noun	+	prep. with pron.
		casus pendens		+	subj.	+	pred.

The interesting thing is that although the second colon opens in a way that signals a syntax completely parallel to the first (participle + genitive), that pattern breaks down with the addition of *mḥth lw*. The sound patterns imitate the grammatical parallelism in that both 'break down' at the same point—at the 'breaking' (*meḥittâ lô*) of the babbler, as the next diagram indicates:

1. Boström, *Paronomasi*, p. 139.

a.	*nōṣēr pîw*	*šōmēr napšô*
	nōṣēr p	*šōmēr n pšô*
b.	*pōśēq śᵉpātāy w*	*mᵉḥittâ lô*
	pōśē ś p	
	t	*tt ô*

In this way, too, attention is focused on the concluding *mḥth lw*.

Proverbs 16.17. The poetic pair *šmr* and *nṣr* is found in the second colon of this proverb.

a.	*mᵉsillat yᵉšārîm sûr mērā'*	The road of the upright means the avoidance of misfortune;
b.	*šōmēr napšô nōṣēr darkô*	one who guards his life is one who watches his way.

One of the differences between the second colon of this proverb and the nearly identical sentence found in the first colon of Prov. 13.3 is the use of *darkô* instead of *pîw* after *nṣr*. The use of *darkô* was meant to parallel the first word *mᵉsillat*. In the first colon there is the juxtaposition of the nominal phrase *mslt yšrym* with the infinitive construct phrase *swr mr'*. The association of the two phrases was meant to affirm not merely that in taking 'the road of the just' one will, *as a consequence*, stay clear of misfortune but, more emphatically and metaphorically, 'the road of the just' *is* the avoidance of misfortune—an inanimate entity (*mᵉsillat*) *is* an action (*sûr*).[1]

The nominal construction, *swr mr'*, is also a ready parallel to its complement in the following colon, *šmr npšw*. The avoidance of misfortune is only the other side of the coin of guarding one's life. This creates a chiastic parallelism for the proverb, which includes a semantic- (*mslt* // *drkw*) sonant (*swr mr'* // *šmr*) chiasmus within it:

a.	*mslt yšrym*	*swr mr'*
	mslt	*s r mr*
	A	B
b.	*šmr npšw*	*nṣr drkw*
	šmr	*drkw*
	B′	A′

In such a case as this where the coordinations in the cola are coupled

1. Cf. Hermisson, *Studien*, pp. 144-45, who names 16.17a as an example of the 'simple coordinating equation'.

with synonymous parallelism between the cola, the bonds between the terms multiply. For now *mslt yšrym* is to be identified not only with *swr mr'* by reason of the coordination, but also with *nṣ drkw* by reason of the chiasmus. And because of this last tie, *mslt yšrym* is also related to *šmr npšw*. In other words, all the terms in the proverb are related.

The sound patterns in the proverb clearly reinforce these relationships. The sibilant and /r/ sounds are repeated through both cola:

a. *mslt yšrym swr mr'* b. *šmr npšw nṣr drkw*
s šr s r r *š r š ṣr r*

Especially noteworthy is the correspondence between the verbal forms *swr, šmr* and *nṣr* because of the sibilant and /r/ sequence in each.[1] In addition these same sounds mark off and emphasize both sides of the coordination in each colon:

a. *msḷt yšrym swr mr'* b. *šmr npšw nṣr drkw*
ms šr s r mr *šmr n š nṣr r*

In each colon it is a combination of nasal, sibilant, and liquid (/r/) sounds that forms the sound pattern. But the combination of /n/ or /m/ with the previously noted sibilant and /r/ pattern also creates a linking pattern. Beginning with *yšrym*, the /ś, r, m/ sequence there is picked up by /s, r, m, r/ of the next two words (*swr mr'*) and by *šmr*, the consonants of the first word of the second colon, which repeat the consonants of *yšrym*. A different nasal, /n/, is introduced with *npšw*, but in the next word it too combines with a sibilant and /r/ in *nṣr*.

a. *mslt yšrym swr mr'* b. *šmr npšw nṣr drkw*
šr m s r mr *šmr*
n š nṣr

Even more, the two cola are also linked by assonance: the /er/ motif in both *mērā'* and *šōmēr*.[2] Finally, the coordination in the second colon is reinforced by an identical sequence of vowels:

b. *šōmēr napšô nōṣēr darkō*
ō ē a ô ō ē a ō

1. Boström, *Paronomasi*, p. 164.
2. Boström, *Paronomasi*, p. 164.

Proverbs 19.8. This is another example of the coordinating proverb, composed of three participial phrases.

a.	*qōneh lēb 'ōhēb napšô*	One who gains understanding is one who is concerned for his well-being;
b.	*šōmēr t^e^bûnâ limṣō' ṭôb*	one who guards knowledge surely finds success.

The unusual factor in this particular line-up of participles is the non-participial final phrase, *limṣō' ṭôb*. The change from the participial format at this point is probably intended to signal the final statement of the proverb.[1] The footnotes in *BHK* and *BHS* would change *limṣō'* to *yimṣā'*. However, the infinitive form with *lamed* is defensible as it stands. It can be used as the predicate of a nominal sentence with the nuance 'is due to, must, will certainly', a stronger statement than simply *yimṣā'*.[2] The MT form also fits into the sound patterning. The form *lmṣ'* continues the /o/ assonance of the proverb and in combination with *ṭôb* echoes the /l, b/ sequence at the beginning of the proverb:

a.	*qōneh lēb . . .*	b.	*. . . limṣō' ṭôb*
	ō l b		*l ō ôb*

Clearly, this kind of patterning is lost (or ignored) by a change to *yimṣā'*.

To illustrate the sound patterning more fully: the basic sounds throughout the proverb are the /o/ vowel (generally long, middle in *limṣō'*) and labials (mostly /n/). Then, combined with other sounds, these form similar patterns in both halves of each colon. Thus, the first colon appears this way:

a.	*qōneh lēb*	*'ōhēb napšô*
	ōn ēb	*ō ēb n ô*

There is the additional assonance of the long /o/ plus /e/ pattern of both participles, *qōneh* and *'ōhēb*, and the motif /eb/ joining both *lēb* and *'ōhēb*.[3] The patterns in the second colon mark off subject and predicate.

1. See Prov. 20.19, Chapter 6.

2. Joüon, *Grammaire*, §154.d; G. Bergsträsser, *Hebräische Grammatik* (Hildesheim: Georg Olms, 1962), II, §11.o.

3. Boström, *Paronomasi*, p. 175.

b. *šōmēr tᵉbûnâ* *limṣō' ṭôb*
šōm t b *mṣō ṭôb*

In addition, just as the beginning and end of the proverb are joined by sounds (as pointed out above), the two middle words, *napšô* and *šōmēr*, are linked by the alliterative repetition of the syllable /*šô*/ in both.[1] And all the participles are linked by the common long /o/ plus /e/ vowel pattern in each.

On the semantic level the same links are operative by reason of the synonymous parallelism between the cola. 'Gaining' (*qōneh*) and 'keeping' (*šōmēr*) understanding, therefore, are related like two sides of the one coin. In turn, 'gaining success' (*limṣō' ṭôb*) is equally true of *qōneh lēb*, as is self-profit (*'ōhēb napšô*) of *šōmēr tᵉbûnâ*. The proverb exposes many facets of a particular reality, rather than sums it up in a concise definition.

Proverbs 12.1. Sometimes the proverbial coordination involves repetition of the participle of the same verb to reinforce the connection. Such a coordination follows the pattern (A + B) = (A + C), where A represents the repeated participle, while B and C represent the elements being matched. In this proverb the (A + B) = (A + C) pattern is in the first colon.

a. *'ōhēb mûsār 'ōhēb dā'at* (A + B) = (A + C)	One who loves correction is one who loves knowledge,
b. *wᵉśōnē' tôkaḥat bā'ar*	but one who hates discipline is a brute!

The repetition and coordination of the two participial phrases reinforce the sense that 'knowledge' is a function of 'correction, discipline', and that they go together. This relationship of ideas is a bit paradoxical as well. No one really *loves* discipline; but if one really loves knowledge, in seeking it one must come to love discipline. Further analysis shows that *'ōhēb mûsār* from the first colon is antithetically paralleled in the second colon by the phrase *śōnē' tôkaḥat*. But then, rather than ending with a fourth participial phrase, the second colon changes this pattern with an abrupt oneword predicate, *bā'ar*, 'a brute'. The unexpected shift in construction focuses attention on *b'r*, underscores the contrast and indicates the conclusion of the proverb.[2]

1. Boström, *Paronomasi*, p. 175.
2. See Prov. 20.19, Chapter 6.

Assonance plays the major role in the sound patterns of the proverb and reflects the semantic structure. Thus, the first colon reflects the semantic coordination by the participial vowel format of long /o/ with /e/, followed in each case by /a/ vowels. The second colon repeats the /o, e/ pattern with *śōnē'*, but the remaining sounds are /a/ vowels, leading into the final word *bā'ar*.

a.	*'ōhēb mûsār*	*'ōhēb dā'at* (< *a't*)
	ō ē ā	*ō ē ā a*
b.	*weśōnē' tôkaḥat* (< *aḥt*)	*bā'ar* (< *a'r*)
	ō ē ô a a	*ā a*

The last words in each colon have the same phonic pattern, consisting of /a/ vowels flanking a /'/: *dā'at* and *bā'ar*.[1] But *dā'at* also echoes *tôkaḥat* in the second colon by reason of dental repetition (/d/ and /t/) and the additional pattern /a, (', ḥ), a/ in both words. Thus *'ōhēb dā'at* is related by sounds to both halves of the second colon:

a.	*'ōhēb mûsār'*	*'ōhēb dā'at* (< *da't*)
		ō ē dā'at
b.	*weśōnē' tôkaḥat* (< *aḥt*)	*bā'ar* (< *a'r*)
	ō ē t aḥat	*ā'a*

Proverbs 19.16. The (A + B) = (A + C) structure can also be found in the first colon of this proverb.

a.	*šōmēr miṣwâ*		*šōmēr napšô*	One who guards precepts is one
	(A + B)	=	(A + C)	who guards his life;
b.	*bôzēh derākāyw*[2]		*yāmût*	one who despises his ways will die.

The repetition of the participle *šōmēr* emphasizes the simple coordination of the colon: obedience = life. The second colon imitates the pattern of the previous proverb (12.1) and substitutes one word for a fourth participial phrase, the verb *yāmût*. The change in pattern

1. Boström, *Paronomasi*, p. 133.

2. *derākāyw* (so all versions) is felt by some to be an inadequate parallel for *miṣwâ*. Dahood (*Proverbs*, pp. 40-41) and Barucq (*Le livre*, p. 156) connect *drkyw* with Ug. *drkt* meaning 'dominion, power, authority'. This sense of Heb. *drk* is accepted, albeit with a question mark, for some OT occurrences by *HALAT*, p. 223, but not for the present text. Others regard final *yw* as dittographic and read *dbr* for *drk*: Toy, *A Critical Commentary*, p. 375; Gemser, *Sprüche*, p. 77; *BHK* and *BHS* agree on the basis of the *dbr–mṣwh* parallel in Prov. 13.13.

draws attention to the contrast in meaning and concludes the proverb.[1]

There are sound patterns as well. Besides the /o, e/ vowel assonance joining the three participles of the proverb, there is sibilant + nasal + /r/ consonance in the first colon that joins both halves of that colon. There is also an alliteration in /šō/ that opens and closes the colon in the words *šōmēr* and *napšô*. The sibilants form a link as far as *bzh* in the second colon, where the /bôz/ sounds of *bwzh* also alliterate with the /p, šô/ of *napšô*. Then the /m/ and /r/ consonance from the first colon is picked up by the last two words of the second colon, *drkyw* and *ywmt*, and there is a dental link between these same words.

a.	*šōmēr mṣwh*	*šōmēr npšô*	b.	*bôzh*	*drkyw*	*ywmt*
	ō ē	*ō ē*				
	š m r mṣ	*š m r n š*			*r*	*m*
	šō	*šō pšô*		*bôz*		
					d	*t*

If *dbr*, however, is accepted as the correct reading in the text instead of *drk*, this change provides an additional phonic link, /b/, which joins *npšw* and *bwzh* with *dbr*. These links give a very marked sound pattern between the two phrases:

a.	. . . *šōmēr napšô*	b.	*bôzh dābār*
	šō r pšô		*bôz b r*

It is to be noted that none of the other sound patterns are lost. Thus, sound patterning in this proverb supplies a supplementary argument in favor of the emendation of *drk(yw)* to *dbr*.

Proverbs 17.19. Another example of this (A + B) = (A + C) pattern again involves the root *'hb*.

a.	*'ōhēb pešaʻ*		*'ōhēb maṣṣâ*	One who loves giving offense is one
	(A + B)	=	(A + C)	who loves strife;
b.	*magbîah pitḥô mᵉbaqqeš šāber*			one who elevates his doorway is one who courts disaster.

This four-participle proverb has coordination in both cola, but only the first follows the (A + B) = (A + C) pattern. In this particular proverb, therefore, there are three relationships: the two halves of

1. See Prov. 20.19, Chapter 6.

each colon to each other, and the intercola semantic parallelism.[1] The image, *mgbyh ptḥw*, is uncertain. It has been understood as a picturesque ellipsis for such phrases as *ptḥy pyk* (Mic. 7.5), *ptḥwn ph* (Ezek. 16.63; 29.21), and verbal *ptḥ* with *ph* as object (Prov. 24.7; see a similar expression, *dl śpty*, in Ps. 141.3; for *g^{e}bōhâ* in the sense of ‘haughty speech’, see 1 Sam. 2.3).[2] In any event, the interlinear parallelism of the proverb probably indicates that *mgbyh ptḥw* is making the sense of *’hb pš‘* more precise.

a.	*’hb pš‘*	*’hb mṣh*
	A	B
b.	*mgbyh ptḥw*	*mbqš šbr*
	A′	B′

The semantic coordination in both cola is paralleled on the level of sound:

a.	*’ōhēb pš‘*	*’ōhēb mṣh*
	’ōhēb š	*’ōhēb ṣ*
b.	*mgbyh ptḥw*	*mbqš šbr*
	mgb p	*mbq b*

The first three participial phrases are linked by labials and the /o/ vowel, and they contain the main sounds of the proverb. The last participial phrase has its own internal chiastic pattern of consonants:[3]

b.	*. . . mbqš šbr*
	b š šb

The intercola sound patterning is equally strong, marked mainly by labials and sibilants.

a.	*’ōhb pš‘*	*’ōhb mṣh*	b.	*mgbyh ptḥô*	*mbqš šbr*
	ō b pš	*ō b mṣ*		*m b p ô*	*mb š šb*

Proverbs 21.23. This next example shows how coordination in proverbs can be expanded from the colon to the whole saying.[4]

a.	*šōmēr pîw ûl^{e}šônô*	One who guards his mouth and tongue—
b.	*šōmēr miṣṣārôt napšô*	one who guards his life from troubles.

1. Hermisson, *Studien*, p. 147.
2. Gemser, *Sprüche*, p. 73.
3. Boström, *Paronomasi*, pp. 169-70.
4. Hermisson, *Studien*, p. 146.

The whole proverb takes the form (A + B) = (A + C) where A represents the repeated *šōmēr*, and B and C represent the elements being associated with *šōmēr*. The saying is then constructed on the pattern: subject (A + B) and predicate (A + C).

a.	*šmr*		*pyw wlšwnw*
	A	+	B
b.	*šmr*		*mṣrwt npšw*
	A	+	C

The effect of this repetition of participles and coordination of phrases is to emphasize the theme of the saying, namely, how close a connection there is between the mouth and tongue, and the well-being of an individual's life.

Sound patterns exercise a strong unifying force in the proverb. There is a clear assonance of /o/ vowels throughout, plus an end rhyme in /ô/, and the consonance of nasals and sibilants as well:

a.	*šmr pyw wlšwnw*	b.	*šmr mṣrwt npšw*
	šm *š n*		*šm* *n š*

The first part of each half of the proverb uses sibilants and /m/; the second part, sibilants and /n/. A few more of these sounds combine in a striking alliteration involving the syllable /šo/, which links both ends of each colon:[1]

a.	*šōmēr pîw ûlešônô*	b.	*šōmēr miṣṣārôt napšô*
	šō *šô*		*šō* *šô*

Proverbs 13.24. This proverb uses assonance in /o/ as the dominant motif in the sound patterning. A tagging sound pattern marks the coordination in the first colon.

a.	*ḥôśēk šibṭô śônē' benô*	One who spares his rod is one who hates his son,
b.	*we'ōhabô šiḥarô mûsār*	but one who loves him is one who eagerly seeks discipline for him.

In the first colon the /o/ vowel frames and distinguishes both subject and predicate by appearing in the first and last syllables of each phrase: *ḥôśēk šibṭô* and *śônē' benô*. But the grammatical and semantic coordination being made between *ḥôśēk* and *śônē'* is highlighted by the recurrence of the /o, e/ vowel sequence of the participial forms

1. Boström, *Paronomasi*, p. 187.

themselves. A coordination in terms of sound is thus also created for the first colon.

a. *ḥôśēk šibṭô śōnē' b^{e}nô*
ô ē ô ô ē' ô
ś šb ś n bn

The sibilants, /b/ and /n/ in the first colon complement this vowel pattern with a linking subpattern of consonance. In the second colon /o/ again unites the subject *'ōh^{a}bô* and the predicate *šiḥ^{a}rô*. And a sequence /(š, s), r/ links *šiḥ^{a}rô* to its object *mûsār*.

b. *w^{e}'ōh^{a}bô šiḥ^{a}rô mûsār*
ō ô ô
š r s r

The /o/ assonance links six of the seven words in the proverb together, creating a phonic harmony throughout. The /b/ of *'ōh^{a}bô*, *šibṭô*, and *b^{e}nô* is another subordinate link between the cola, as is the /ši/ motif in *šibṭô* and *šiḥ^{a}rô*. But all these phonic links contrast with the antithetic parallelism between the cola. That is, while the sound patterns in this proverb are busy interrelating words, the sense structure is busy contrasting them. And so the parallelism, in chiastic form, produces the following structure:

a.	*ḥôśēk šibṭô*	*śōnē' b^{e}nô*
	A	B
b.	*w^{e}'ōh^{a}bô*	*šiḥ^{a}rô mûsār*
	B′	A′

'Drawing back from' (*ḥôśēk*) is contrasted with 'eagerly seeking out' (*šiḥ^{a}rô*), and 'hating' (*śōnē'*) with 'loving' (*'ōh^{a}bô*). But an even more interesting parallel is between *šibṭô* and *mûsār*. 'Discipline', the proverb is suggesting, is more than a matter of words, and 'punishment' can be 'love'.

2. *Proverbs Using Imagery*

Introduction

The coordinating structure is often used in proverbs that use imagery to express 'some similarity or analogy' between things.[1] These

1. S. Ullmann, *Language and Style* (Oxford: Basil Blackwell, 1964), p. 177;

expressions in Hebrew are commonly indicated by the correlative particles *ka'ᵃšer*, 'as, in the same way', *kᵉ*, 'like, as', or *kēn*, 'so, thus'. However, in coordinating proverbs the particles are dropped and the relationship is expressed simply by placing the items involved side by side in the sentence as, for example, in Jer. 17.11:[1]

qōrē' dāgar wᵉlō' yālād	A partridge that gathers together off-spring not her own—
'ōšeh 'ōšer wᵉlō' bᵉmišpāṭ	whoever acquires wealth unjustly.

Such coordination can be found within a colon (intracolon) or between cola (intercola) as is the case with the sayings found in Proverbs 25–27. The first proverb given below is an example of intracola coordination.

Texts

Proverbs 12.6. Coordination occurs in the first colon only.

a.	*dibrê rᵉšā'îm 'ᵉrob dām*	The words of the wicked—a bloody ambush,
b.	*ûpî yᵉšārîm yaṣṣîlēm*	but the mouth of the upright offers safety.

The infinitival phrase is obviously imagery, with the referent boldly set down beside it in the colon, but with no further indications of the relationship between them. The colon means that, 'The words of the wicked are a bloody ambush', a metaphor combining otherwise incompatible things: 'words' and 'ambushes'. The underlying correspondence between 'words' and 'ambushes' is highlighted by their simply being placed side by side.

The sound pattern in the first colon emphasizes the semantic coordination. Four consonants from *dbry rš'ym* are repeated in reverse in the second half of the colon.[2]

a.	*dbry rš'ym*	*'rb dm*
	dbr r m	*rb dm*

Thus, the image *'rb dm* is associated with its referent (*dbry rš'ym*) by sound. The sound pattern in the second colon is just as prominent

Hermisson (*Studien*, p. 58) also distinguishes these as 'Vergleichssprüche'.

1. Joüon, *Grammaire*, §174.h; D.F. Payne, 'A Perspective on the Use of Simile in the Old Testament', *Semitics* 1 (1970), p. 112; Delitzsch (*Biblical Commentary*, VI.1, p. 9) calls this latter type of proverb 'emblematic', to distinguish it from those that use the correlatives and that he names 'comparisons'.

2. Boström, *Paronomasi*, p. 134.

and marks off the subject and the predicate of the colon by the repetition of the same sounds.

b. *wpî yšrîm* *yṣîlm*
î yš îm *yṣî m*

Both halves of each colon are joined by sound. The cola, too, are connected by the alliteration in the antithetic word pair, 'wicked' and 'upright':[1]

r^ešā'îm / *r^ešā -îm*
y^ešā rîm / - *^ešārîm*

The proverb, consequently, proves to be a tightly woven structure of sound and sense.

There is one final problem—the antecedent for the suffix on *yṣylm* in the second colon. The obvious sense of the parallelism in the proverb is that the wicked attack people (first colon) and, on the other hand, the upright save them (second colon).[2] Such being the case, the suffix cannot refer to the *rš'ym* in the first colon and, thus, it has no antecedent in that colon. This would leave *yšrym* in the second colon as the only possible antecedent. But the parallelism does not support this either since the *yšrym* are probably portrayed as saving *others*. Toy chooses to delete the suffix.[3] But the multiple instances of sound patterning in this proverb, into which the suffix on *yṣylm* fits in a number of ways, indicates that /m/ is to be maintained, possibly as an enclitic *mem*.

Proverbs 11.22. With this proverb a section illustrating intercola coordination of imagery begins.

a. *nezem zāhāb b^e'ap ḥ^azîr* A gold ring in a swine's snout—
b. *'iššâ yāpâ w^esārat ṭā'am* a woman beautiful but lacking discretion.

The proverb makes its point by the confrontation between the two pictures: the swine's ring and the beautiful but thoughtless woman. Not a word is added to explain the relationship between them. The comparison is achieved by the simple alignment of both pictures, one in each colon, colon a being predicated of colon b. The burlesque image itself

1. Boström, *Paronomasi*, p. 134.
2. Toy, *A Critical Commentary*, p. 244.
3. Toy, *A Critical Commentary*, p. 244.

is quite forceful, based as it is 'on the world as it patently is *not*'.[1] Pigs do not wear gold! Neither should beauty be without discretion!

The sound patterning reflects the correspondence between both cola. The main sounds in the first colon are /z/ and /(b, p)/. These are echoed in the second colon by other sibilants and /p/.

a. *nzm zhb b'p ḥzyr* b. *'šh yph wsrt ṭ'm*
z z b b p z *š p s*

Particularly significant is the way the /z/ and labial sounds tie the 'gold ring' and 'swine' together and then both are echoed by *'šh yph* in the next colon. These are the main terms in the comparison and link both images. But the relationships between the sounds are even more elaborate.

a. *nzm zhāb b'ap ḥzyr* b. *'šâ yāpâ wsrt ṭ'm*
āb b ap z r *āp sr*

The *'iššâ yāpâ* phrase is also linked to the first colon by the way /āpâ/ from *yāpâ* echoes the /ap/ of *bᵉ'ap* and the /ab/ in *zāhāb*. The word *sārat* in the latter half of the second colon also echoes the second half of the first colon, particularly the word *ḥᵃzîr*, because of the /r/ and sibilants in both.[2] The bond between both cola is forged not only by the imagery but also by the sounds.

The peculiar appropriateness of the words chosen for this proverb becomes even clearer if the proverb were to be rewritten in the following fashion (maintaining the same meaning):

nezem ketem bᵉ'ap ḥᵃzîr
'ēšet yᵒpî bᵉlî ṭā'am

In this version the sound patterns of the original are destroyed even though the variations are slight. The second colon now has little to tie it to the first colon.

Proverbs 17.3 and 27.21. These two proverbs, which will be studied together because of their identical first cola, have the appearance of a list of metaphors which lead up to a concluding application.

1. Payne, 'A Perspective', p. 116.
2. Boström, *Paronomasi*, p. 131.

a. *maṣrēp lakkesep w^{e}kûr lazzāhāb*	A crucible for silver and a furnace for gold
b. *ûbōḥēn libbôt* YHWH	and the tester of hearts is the Lord (Prov. 17.3).

a. *maṣrēp lakkesep w^{e}kûr lazzāhāb*	A crucible for silver and a furnace for gold
b. *w^{e}'îš l^{e}pî mah^{a}lālô*	and a man, by the praise he receives (Prov. 27.21).

Although each proverb has nearly the same appearance there are significant syntactic and semantic differences which must be analysed.

With the first proverb (17.3) the predicate, which is given explicitly in the second colon (*bōḥēn*), must be understood in the first. Keeping that in mind the syntactic and semantic relationships in this proverb can be diagrammed as follows:

a.	*mṣrp*		*(bḥn)*	*lksp*			*wkwr*		*(bḥn)*	*lzhb*		
semantic:	'tester'		+	'tested'		/	'tester'		+	'tested'		
syntax:	noun	+	(part.)	+ prep. +	obj.	/	noun	+	(part.)	+ prep. +	obj.	
	Subj.			Pred.			Subj.			Pred.		

b.	*wbḥn*		*lbwt*		YHWH
semantic:			'tested'	+	tester
syntax:	part.	+	gen.	+	proper name
		Pred.		+	Subj.

Both cola have active predicates, the one in the first colon being implied. The prepositional phrase of the first colon is also replaced in the second colon by the genitival relationship of *libbôt* to the participle. In addition, the order of subject and predicate in the second colon is reversed from the first colon. The semantic structure follows the syntax in both cola: in each case the 'tester' is associated with the subject and the 'tested' with the predicate, even reversing its order in the second colon to match the reversed syntax there as well. Semantically and syntactically, therefore, the structures of the cola in 17.3 are the same chiastic formation:

a.	*mṣrp*		*lksp*		*wkwr*		*lzhb*
	(A	+	B)	+	(A′	+	B′)
b.	*wbḥn lbwt*				YHWH		
	B″		+		A″		

Prov. 27.21 is different. In this proverb the predicate must be understood in both cola but the sense of 'testing' seems appropriate still.

a.	*mṣrp*	(*bḥn*)	*lksp*	*wkwr*	(*bḥn*)	*lzhb*
semantic:	'tester'	+	'tested'	/ 'tester'	+	'tested'
syntax:	noun +	(part.) +	prep. + obj.	/ noun +	(part.) +	prep. + obj.
	Subj.	Pred.		Subj.	Pred.	

b.	*w'yš*	(*ybḥn*)	*lpy*	*mhllw*
semantic:	'tested'		+	'tester'
syntax:	noun +	(pass. v.) +	prep. +	obj.
	Subj.	Pred.		

Each colon retains the same order of subject and predicate and the prepositional phrase is used in each. In the first colon, however, the predicate has an active sense and in the second colon a passive sense. This difference places the semantic and syntactic structures at odds with each other in the second colon. The 'tested' becomes the noun in the subject position and the predicate becomes the 'tester'. Semantically, therefore, 27.21b is the same as 17.3b where the order of 'tested' and 'tester' is reversed from the first colon.

a.	*mṣrp*		*lksp*		*wkwr*		*lzhb*	
	(A	+	B)	+	(A′	+	B′)	
b.	*w'yš*				*lpy mhllw*			
	B″		+		A″			

But the syntactic structure of 27.21b is the same as its first colon (27.21a) and so this proverb differs from the syntax of 17.3b by reason of the implied passive in 27.21b.

a.	*mṣrp*		*lksp*		*wkwr*		*lzhb*
	(Subj.	+	Pred.)	+	(Subj	+	Pred.)
b.	*w'yš*				*lpy mhllw*		
	Subj.		+		Pred.		

On the semantic level, therefore, each proverb has the same general structure: once having established a pair of metaphors in the first colon, the proverb moves, in the second colon, to the level of human life and value judgments simply by the use of the conjunction.[1] The semantic chiasmus in each proverb creates a bit of suspense by placing last the word (*YHWH* and *mhllw*) that corresponds to the first-mentioned item in each metaphor (*mṣrp* and *kwr*). It is this last word

1. This conjunction is called the *waw adaequationis*—Joüon, *Grammaire*, §174.h; GKC, §611.aN.

that the writer of each proverb especially wishes to emphasize.

The phonic pattern of each proverb simply underscores the relationship between metaphors and applications. The first colon coordinates the two images by the use of sibilants, labials, /l/ and /k/:

a.	*mṣrp lksp*	*wkwr lzhb*
	ṣrp lksp	*k r lz b*

The first image is closely tied together by the same consonance of sibilants and /p/:

a.	*mṣrp lksp . . .*
	ṣ p sp

The first words of each image are linked by /r/: *mṣrp* and *kwr*. The coordination between cola is also reflected in sound. The second colon of 17.3 echoes the labials and /l/ of the first colon and maintains a /bo/ alliteration between *bōḥen* and *libbôt*.

17.3a.	*mṣrp lksp*	*wkwr lzhb*	b.	*ûbōḥēn*	*libbôt* YHWH
	p l p	*l b*		*b*	*l bb*
				bō	*bô*

The sibilants as well as the labials and /l/ of the first colon are echoed by 27.21b:

27.21a.	*mṣrp lksp*	*wkwr lzhb*	b.	*w'yš lpy mhllw*
	ṣ p l sp	*lz b*		*š lp ll*

Proverbs 25.11. This proverb is about the power of the spoken word.

a.	*tappûḥê zāhāb b*^{e}*maśkiyyôt kāsep*	Golden apricots in silver settings—
b.	*dābār dābūr 'al 'opnāyw*[1]	a word spoken in its proper form.

1. The phrase *'al 'opnāyw* is uncertain, but is usually understood to refer to 'proper time' or 'circumstances'—'at the proper time' (NAB); 'fitly' (Toy, *A Critical Commentary*, p. 462); 'according to its circumstances' (Delitzsch, *Biblical Commentary*, VI.2, p. 155); 'zu seiner Zeit' (Gemser, *Sprüche*, p. 113); and 'à propos' (Barucq, *Le livre*, p. 194). But Boström (*Paronomasi*, p. 51; see *HALAT*, p. 76) notes the use of *'wpnym* in Sir. 50.27 in connection with *mšl*, and suggests that the word is an expression for the form of the proverb. McKane (*Proverbs*, p. 584) takes up this suggestion and tentatively explains the form as dual and as due 'to the compact elegance of expression produced by the balancing halves of a wisdom sentence'. The suggestion is an attractive one with respect to this proverb because the imagery of the first colon speaks of valuable things placed in enhancing settings. The comparable 'setting' for a word or expression would be its form—the

Image and application are simply lined up next to one another, colon a being predicated of colon b. Though without any expression of comparison or similitude included to make precise the relationship, the mere coordination of cola makes the comparison obvious. The specific terms involved that manifest semantic and grammatical parallelism are: *tappûhê zāhāb* and *dābār dābūr; b^{e}maśkiyyôt kāsep* and *'al 'opnāyw*. Sound patterns of dentals and labials join the cola:

a.	*tpwḥy zhb bmśkywt ksp*	b.	*dbr dbr 'l 'pnyw*
	tp b b t p		*db db p*

The additional sounds of sibilants in the first colon mark off both parts of the imagery and there is, besides, chiasmus in the last two words of the first colon:

a.	*tpwḥy zhb*	*bmśkywt ksp*
	tp z b	*b ś t sp*
		b śk ksp

Proverbs 25.12. This proverb uses the imagery of precious metalwork to describe the power of the spoken word.

a.	*nezem zāhāb wah^{a}lî kātem*	A gold earring and an ornament of fine gold—
b.	*môkîaḥ ḥākām 'al 'ōzen šōmā'at*	a wise rebuker of an attentive ear.

The pattern again is the simple coordination of images with colon a being predicated of colon b. Gold earrings and ornaments that enhance the ears of the wearer (understood) are compared to the wise teacher whose training for attentive ears improves the ears (again understood) and now by metonymy referring to the whole person. The semantic parallelism is to be analysed this way:

a.	*nzm zhb*	*wḥly ktm*
	A	A′
b.	*mwkyḥ ḥkm 'l 'zn šm't*	
	A″	

The grammatical structure is as follows:

a.	*nzm*		*zhb*		*wḥly*		*ktm*		
	noun	+	adj.	+	noun	+	gen.	=	Pred.
b.	*mwkyḥ*		*ḥkm*		*'l 'zn šm't*				
	noun	+	adj.	+	obj. of v.			=	Subj.

word spoken in a pleasing and appealing way. The exact meaning of the expression remains obscure.

The presence of the phrase *'l 'zn šm't* in the second colon prevents the presence of complete grammatical parallelism in the proverb. On the level of sound, however, each side of the comparison displays parallel patterns, arranged chiastically.

Because of the close association between this proverb and the previous one, Toy wants to change the rarer *ketem* in the first colon to *kesep* (thus matching the *zāhāb . . . kesep* pair in 25.11a); and change *mwkyḥ* to *twkḥt* (thus more closely paralleling the *dābār* of 25.11b).[1] An important argument against such a move is the sound patterning.[2] *Ketem* was clearly chosen over either *zāhāb, ḥārûṣ* or *kesep* because of its ability to join both cola of the proverb by sound. The /ḥ/ of *ḥly*, together with the /k/ and /m/ of *ktm*, are echoed chiastically in *mwkḥ*; just as consonants of the first two words of the second colon (*mwkḥ ḥkm*) also echo chiastically, thus:

a. *nzm zhb wḥly ktm*	b. *mwkḥ ḥkm 'l 'zn šm't*
ḥ k m	*m kḥ ḥkm*

The beginning and end of the proverb are joined by the letters /n/ and /z/, with /š/ of *šm't* in place of the second /z/ for the second colon. A chiastic sound pattern, consequently, is constructed which makes the equation between image and application hard and fast:

a. *nzm zhb wḥly ktm*	b. *mwkḥ ḥkm 'l 'zn šm't*
nz z	*zn š*
ḥ k m	*m kḥ ḥkm*

These last two proverbs are not the easiest to interpret with certainty. They still leave unanswered questions. The problems are partially lexical and partially due to the compactness of proverbial style. The preceding analysis, nonetheless, shows clear sound patterning interwoven into the texts as they stand. Such patterns argue against solutions built on emendation, at least of the consonantal text.

Proverbs 25.23.

a. *rûaḥ ṣāpôn tᵉḥôlēl gāšem*	The north wind brings forth rain—
b. *ûpānîm niz'āmîm lᵉšôn sāter*	and angry faces, the dissembling tongue.

The precise interpretation of this proverb is difficult and debatable.

1. Toy, *A Critical Commentary*, pp. 463, 466.
2. Boström, *Paronomasi*, p. 76.

The problems center on the imagery in the first colon where the *rûaḥ ṣāpôn* is presented as bringing rain. This does not fit the climatic conditions of Palestine where it is the west wind that brings the rain (1 Kgs 18.43-45; Lk. 12.54); the north wind is the one which clears the air after a storm.[1] To solve the difficulty Dalman suggests that the verb *tḥwll* is emphasizing the aspect of 'pain', rather than 'birth', so that the first colon would mean, 'The north wind frightens the rainstorm', hindering it from coming.[2] The basis of the comparison with the second colon would simply be that both the north wind and the secretive tongue cause evil. Another commentator interprets *ṣpwn* as 'hidden' (*ṣāpûn*). In this view, the rain-bearing wind is from a secret, unknown source and thus can be compared to the slander, the origin of which is unknown, but which, nonetheless, has its visible effect on the face of its victim.[3] The basis of the comparison here can be explained as secret cause, visible effect. Each of these translations, however, seems forced. A simpler solution, perhaps, is to assume that *rwḥ ṣpwn* is the northwest wind, justifying, thereby, its association with rain.[4] OT Hebrew has no words for the intermediate points of the compass.

On the structural level, the proverb is chiastically arranged so that its main emphasis and the source of the 'angry faces' is mentioned last: 'the dissembling tongue'. The terms that are grammatically related are:

a.	*rwḥ ṣpwn*	*tḥwll*	*gšm*
	subj.	v.	obj.
b.	*wpnym nz'mym*		*lšwn str*
	obj.		subj.

Grammatically, therefore, the parallelism between cola is clear, presenting the coordination in chiastic form. The verb *tḥwll* does double-duty in the second colon. The images in the first colon are related to the terms in the second only because of the coordination of the two cola and the implied comparison resulting from that: the north wind has a similar effect with respect to the rain, as does a lying

1. F.M. Abel, *Géographie de la Palestine* (2 vols.; Paris: Gabalda, 1933), I, p. 119; G. Dalman, *Arbeit und Sitte in Palästina* (7 vols.; Gütersloh: Bertelsmann, 1928–1942), I, p. 246.
2. Dalman, *Arbeit und Sitte*, I, p. 246.
3. J. van der Ploeg, 'Prov xxv 23', *VT* 3 (1953), pp. 189-91.
4. Abel, *Géographie*, I, p. 119; Toy, *A Critical Commentary*, pp. 468-69.

tongue with respect to angry faces. Given one (north wind/deceitful tongue), the other can be expected (rain/angry faces). But the first colon is expressing something positive and beneficial, the second colon, something evil. In this sense, the images of colon a, in relationship to their corresponding terms in colon b, are antithetic.

Sound patterns reinforce the chiastic structure of the coordination, especially the relationship between 'wind' and 'tongue'. These words are bound together by a motif combining /r/, sibilants, and the syllable /ōn/.[1] The other halves of the proverb continue the sibilant consonance, joined to a pattern of nasal consonants.

a. *rwḥ ṣpôn*	*tḥwll gšm*	b. *wpnym nz'mym*	*lšôn ṣtr*
r ṣ ôn			*šôn ṣ r*
	šm	*n m nz m m*	

One last observation: note the consonance between *ṣpwn*, in the first colon, and *pnym*, in the second, by reason of the consonants /p/ and /n/ in both. Such sound patterning, especially the emphasis on *ṣāpôn* and *lešôn*, makes it highly probable that the difficulties with this proverb, for which no really satisfactory solution can yet be offered, do not lie with the correctness of the text.

Proverbs 25.25. This proverb also has a chiastic sound pattern.

a. *mayim qārîm 'al nepeš 'ayēpâ*	Cool waters to a thirsty[2] person
b. *ûšemû'â ṭôbâ mē'ereṣ merḥāq*	and good news from a far land.

Here, because of the *waw adaequationis* (see above) joining the two cola, the grammar of the proverb can be analysed as two nominal sentences (colons a and b) with understood predicates.

a. *mym*	*qrym*	*'l npš 'yph*	(is refreshment)
noun	adj.	adj. phrase	(adj.)
	Subj.		(Pred.)
b. *wšmw'h*	*ṭwbh*	*m'rṣ mrḥq*	(is refreshment)
noun	adj.	adj. phrase	(adj.)
	Subj.		(Pred.)

The grammatical parallelism between the cola is clear. But the

1. Boström, *Paronomasi*, pp. 74-75.

2. Isa. 29.8, Job 22.7 and Ps. 143.6 illustrate the association of *'āyēp*, 'faint, weary', with thirst.

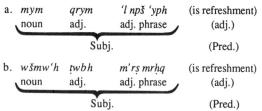

semantic structure (imagery) is different.

a. *mym qrym* — *‘l npš ‘yph*
thing desired + person desiring
image

b. *wšmw‘h ṭwbh* — *m’rṣ mrḥq*
thing desired + source (+ person desiring)
image

On this level the phrase *‘l npš ‘yph* can be considered as being implied in the second colon, but in another sense: it is a non-physical ‘thirst’ for ‘news’. The word *merḥāq*, which describes *šmw‘h ṭwbh*, suggests either *unexpected* news (as news from a distant land might be) or news *anxiously awaited* (as news from a far-off friend would be). In either case, the news would be a source of refreshment and joy (as are the ‘cool waters’).

The sounds of this proverb unmistakably reflect the comparison with matching patterns in each colon arranged chiastically. The first and last halves of the proverb mirror each other by reason of the consonance provided by /m/, /r/ and /q/.[1] The consonants /‘/ and /š/, and the labials /(b, p)/ bind the remaining halves.

a. *mym qrym ‘l npš ‘ypâ*	b. *wšmw‘â ṭwbâ m’rṣ mrḥq*
m m qr m	*m r mr q*
pš ‘ p	*š ‘ b*

A linking pattern between both cola is also provided by the rhyme in /â/, involving *‘^{a}yēpâ* at the end of the first colon, and *ûš^{e}mû‘â ṭôbâ* at the beginning of the second.

Proverbs 26.3. The same technique used in the previous proverb, of listing the pictures side by side, one after the other, is used here also. The listing in this case has a climactic effect.

a. *šôṭ lassûs meteg lah^{a}môr* — A whip for the horse, a bridle for the ass
b. *w^{e}šēbeṭ l^{e}gēw k^{e}sîlîm* — and a rod for the back of fools.

Three pictures are used, the last of which is the one toward which the other two build.

The sound pattern basically follows the same sequence in each

1. Boström, *Paronomasi*, p. 46.

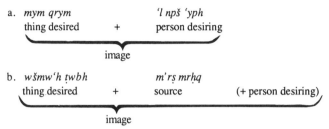

colon, reflecting the coordination between the imagery of the first colon and the imagery of the second. They also create interesting associations in this saying. First, *šôṭ* and *šbṭ* are linked by the consonants /š/ and /ṭ/. The 'fool's back' is linked to 'the bridle for the ass' because of the repetition of /l/ and /g/ in each phrase: *lgw* and *mtg lḥmwr*. Finally, 'fools', *ksylym*, echoes the 'horse', *lsws*, and 'bridle', *mtg*, because of the repetition of /l/, /s/, and /m/,[1] and it echoes the 'ass', *lḥmwr*, because of the repetition of /l/ and /m/ reinforced by the /m/ of *mtg*.

a. *šwṭ lsws mtg lḥmwr*	b. *wšbṭ lgw ksylym*
š ṭ	*š ṭ*
g l	*lg l*
ls s m	*s l m*
m l m	*l l m*

Thus, even on the level of sound, the fool is put on an equal footing with the horse and the ass!

Proverbs 26.14. A phonic chiasmus is present in this saying.

a. *haddelet tissôb ‘al ṣîrāh*	The door turns on its hinge
b. *w^{e}‘āṣēl ‘al miṭṭātô*	and the lazy one on his bed.

This humorous imagery uses word repetition (*‘al*) and sound patterns for reinforcing the comparison. The image is obviously directed toward the *‘ṣl*, and the phrase *‘l ṣyrh* 'was undoubtedly chosen to allude to it'.[2] The allusion is on the basis of the repetition of the consonants in *‘ṣl*. This consonance, plus the repetition of the preposition *‘al*, joins the second half of the first colon with the beginning of the second colon. That, plus the dental consonance between the remaining words, yields a chiastic sound patterning tying the whole proverb together.

a. *hdlt tswb ‘l ṣyrh*	b. *w‘ṣl ‘l mṭṭw*
d t t	*ṭṭ*
‘l ṣ	*‘ṣl ‘l*

1. Boström, *Paronomasi*, p. 77.
2. Boström, *Paronomasi*, p. 78.

Chapter 7

WORDS AND SOUNDS

This investigation of sound patterns in the proverbs has moved gradually from a consideration of elementary patterns of assonance, consonance and alliteration, to more intricate arrangements of sound, such as correlation, linking and tagging patterns. In the process, it has become evident how sound patterns sometimes reinforce the semantic structure of the verse as, for example, in the case of tagging sound patterns, which underscore grammatical or sense units in a line. This chapter will give more evidence for the relationship of sound to sense by studying word repetition and wordplay. Such devices necessarily involve the repetition of the same or similar sounds. At this particular stage of the investigation these topics also provide an opportunity to test further the observations that have been made so far about sound patterns by applying them to other proverbs and in conjunction with other poetic figures.

Actually, repetition as a poetic device has already been studied under one form in the previous chapters. This was the use of sounds in a proverb based on the recurrence of similar or identical consonants and vowels from one word to another in many different but describable patterns. Now the concern will be with the repetition of identical words or word roots within one colon of a proverb or from one colon to the next. Such repetition can involve words with the same or very similar meanings (repetition of words and roots) or the use of identical or like-sounding roots that have different meanings (wordplay). In each case it is meaning as well as sounds that are the significant factors. Word repetition will be studied first.

1. *Word Repetition*

Introduction

The recurrence of the same word or words in successive lines of poetry is a common enough phenomenon, with extremely varied applications. W. Whitman uses it to echo the staccato-like sound of the bugle and the thundering beat of the drum in order to create a mood of relentless and alarming urgency in the following lines of his poem, *Beat! Beat! Drums!*

> Beat! beat! drums! blow! bugles! blow!
> Through the windows—through the doors—burst like a ruthless force,
> Into the solemn church, and scatter the congregation,
> Into the school where the scholar is studying. . .

E.B. Browning repeats the phrase 'I love thee' in almost every line of the poem *How Do I Love Thee?* in order to convey the intensity of her feelings.[1] The repetition of the same word or phrase, at exact and regular intervals, can set off certain segments of a poem and divide a narrative into parts; it can provide a static point against which shifts or developments in thought can be measured.[2] Such is the case with this modern weather proverb:

> Red sky at night, sailor's delight;
> Red sky at morning, sailor's warning.

This contemporary example of antithetic parallelism is structured around three basic elements: (1) word repetition—'red sky' and 'sailor's'; (2) contrast—the word pairs 'night–morning' and 'delight–warning'; and (3) sound patterning—the end rhyme between 'night–delight' and 'morning–warning'. The repetition of 'red sky' and 'sailor's' highlights the ideas being contrasted by serving as an unchanging background against which the elements in tension ('night–morning' and 'delight–warning') stand out.[3] The sound patterning underscores each side of the theme: 'night–delight' and 'morning–warning'.

1. This example is from Brooks and Warren (eds.), *Understanding Poetry*, p. 526.
2. S.F. Fogle, 'Repetition', in Preminger (ed.), *Princeton Encyclopedia of Poetry and Poetics*, p. 699.
3. Fogle, 'Repetition', p. 699.

A similar kind of analysis can be applied to biblical examples of repetition such as Job 1.21.

a. *'ārōm yāṣāṯî mibbeṭen 'immî*
b. *w^e'ārōm 'āšûb šāmmâ*
c. *YHWH nātan waYHWH lāqāḥ*
d. *y^ehî šēm YHWH m^ebōrāk*

Here, too, the same basic elements can be discerned. There is the word repetition in cola a and b of *'ārōm*, 'naked', against which is played off the dual theme of 'going forth' (*yāṣāṯî*) and 'returning' (*'ašûb*). The image refers to the nakedness of the newly born baby ('going forth') and the nakedness of the body ready for the tomb ('returning'). But in view of the severe straits in which Job finds himself, *'ārōm* is much more significant. The nakedness of Job is the nakedness of the mourner clothed only in a mourning garment or in his ripped tunic, and deprived of all he held dear. All the happiness Job once had pales before the present disaster. Overwhelmed by the immensity of the catastrophes that have befallen him, Job claims that the essential nature of his existence has been the same—a naked mourner deprived of all possessions. He was born and has grown old, but nothing has changed: *'ārōm . . . 'ārōm*. His nakedness has only been intensified. The nakedness of his birth is nothing compared with his present nakedness: deprived of wife, children, friends, health, home and possessions. Furthermore, the 'womb' to which Job returns is, of course, that of mother earth (Gen. 2.7; 3.19; Ps. 90.3; Isa. 55.10). Job's reflections are probably meant to echo directly Gen. 3.19 or a similar story, and thus he describes not only his own lot but that of the whole human race.

In cola c and d the name of God is associated with two antithetic activities, *nātan*, 'he gives', and *lāqāḥ*, 'he takes away'. This use of repetition and contrast, plus the similarity of this pattern to the first one (cola a and b), underscores the assertion that God is responsible for Job's absurd and miserable life by his arbitrary and, to all appearances, unjust decisions. Job is naked; God alone is the cause. The third use of the divine name in colon d makes the final statement a shocking about face: 'May the name of God be blessed!' The whole logic of the advance of the argument in the first three cola simply demands: *y^ehî šēm YHWH m^equllāl*, or the like (see Job 1.9-11). The logic of Job the believer is something apart from ordinary logic.

The sound patterns clearly associate this last assertion with what has already been stated.

a. *ʿārōm yāṣātî mibbeṭen ʾimmî*	b. *w*^{e}*ʿārōm ʾāšûb šāmmâ*
ʿārōm	*ʿārōm*
m ṣ m bb mm	*m š b š mm*
c. *YHWH nātan waYHWH lāqāḥ*	d. *yehî šēm YHWH m*^{e}*bōrāk*
YHWH YHWH	*y h YHWH*
	š m m b

Whereas the repetition of *ʿārōm* ties the first pair of cola together (a and b), and the sounds involved in the repetition of *YHWH* join the second pair (c and d), the final colon is related to the first two cola by another sound pattern composed of /m/, /b/ and sibilants. Despite the unique sentiment expressed in the last colon, it is not out of step with the rest of the poem in terms of sound. It is the final, contrasting twist in a poem built upon contrasts.

Proverbial language in the OT bears witness to an equally prolific and varied use of word repetition. After studying the first three of the following proverbs (27.19; 10.9; and 18.3) as instances of word repetition *within* a colon (intracolon repetition), the remaining examples will illustrate repetition of words from one colon to the next (intercola repetition).

Texts

Proverbs 27.19. This example of intracolon repetition is also an example of the striking use of parallelism and an instance of the brevity of language caused by ellipsis.

a. *kammayim happānîm lappānîm*	Like the water (which reflects) the face to the face,
b. *kēn lēb hāʾādām lāʾādām*	so the heart of the man to the man.

The close juxtaposition and repetition of the words in both cola provide a very succinct, even cryptic, statement. Here the proverb will be analysed as follows:

PRED.:	Like the water		(which reflects)	the face		to the face
	kammayim			*happānîm*		*lappānim*
	prep. phrase		+	obj.	+	prep. phrase
	A			B		C
SUBJ.:	so	the heart of the man	(which reflects)	(the man)		to the man
	kēn	*lēb hā'ādām*				*lā'ādām*
	particle +	noun + gen.	+	(obj.)	+	prep. phrase
		A′		(B′)		C′

The basic structure of the proverb is: 'The heart of the man (subj.) is like water (pred.)'. In each colon the relative pronoun is understood and a verb ('reflects' or something similar) is implied. The word in the second colon paralleling *happānîm* is also to be understood (B′, 'the man'), although it does appear as the genitive after *lēb*. The basic sense uniting both clauses, according to this interpretation, is that both *mayim* and *lēb* act as mirrors. *Mayim* reflects the person externally—one's face and looks; *lēb* reflects the person's inner thoughts, desires and feelings. What A/A′ (the mirror) does is to bring B/(B′) and C/C′ together with few words wasted. As only one face seems to be in view in the first colon, so only one person is intended in the second, who, by reflection and introspection, comes to know himself.[1]

The double word repetition is reinforced by similar sound patterning in each colon, underlining the identity of *pnym* and *'dm* as one and the same in each case. The word repetition parallels the imagery—the reflected face equals the real face; the 'reflected' man equals the real man. Besides this, the sounds also associate the first colon with the second by a consonance using the sounds of /k/, /h/, /m/, and /l/.

a.	*kmayim*	*happānîm*	*lappânîm*	b.	*kn*	*lb*	*hā'ādām*	*lā'ādām*
	a im	*appānîm*	*appânîm*				*ā'ādām*	*ā'ādām*
	km	*m h*	*m l*	*m*	*k*	*l*	*h*	*m l* *m*

Furthermore, each word in the first colon has an end rhyme in /im/ and the whole proverb resonates with the sound of /a/ vowels.

The next two cases of word repetition within the colon take a

1. McKane, *Proverbs*, p. 616; Barucq, *Le livre*, p. 216 and n. 9; Scott, *Proverbs*, p. 162.

distinctive form. The colon consists of two terms (subject and predicate) with each term composed of two words. One word in each term is the same, the other words differ. The pattern can be schematized this way: (x + y) (x + z). The pattern illustrates the ability of repetitive devices to build up a sense of expectancy: the anticipated variation creates interest. For example, a certain relationship between 'coming' and 'being served' is established by the word repetition in 'First come, first served'. Word repetition can help contrast opposites which, oddly enough, when looked at from another point of view are really the same: 'Easy come, easy go'. The repetition is enhanced by the simple juxtaposition of phrases without conjunctions, correlatives or modifiers. A sentence like 'The one who comes first is the one to be served first' clutters and somewhat obscures the repetition with needless verbiage. Conciseness is a hallmark of proverbial language, paring down ideas to the essential minimum for comprehension. In this pattern the minimum requirements are the words being repeated and the words being played off against each other.

Proverbs 10.9.

a.	*hôlēk battōm yēlek beṭaḥ* (x + y) (x + z)	One who walks honestly walks securely,
b.	*ûmeʿaqqēš derākāyw yiwwādēaʿ*	but one who makes his ways devious will be discovered.

The relationship between the *hlk* derivatives (x) is not just that of subject to predicate. The subject, *hôlēk battōm,* describes an action, honest living, and the predicate, *yēlek beṭaḥ*, asserts the consequence, security. The repetition of the verbal root furnishes a common background against which that transition from action to consequence, from virtue to reward, can be highlighted. The /lek, b, (t, ṭ)/ alliterative sequence of this colon binds the sentence tightly together as well.

a. *hôlēk btm yēlek bṭḥ*
lēk bt lek bṭ

The second colon, which gives the alternative to virtue and reward, provides a small linking sound pattern for its words.

b. *wm'qš drkyw ywd'*
   q   k
   ' d   d'

These sounds associate the vice, *m'qš drkyw*, with its reward, *ywd'*, 'being found out'.[1]

Proverbs 18.3.

a. *b^e bô' rāšā' bā' gam bûz*	When the wicked person comes,
(x + y) (x + z)	scorn comes too;
b. *w^e 'im qālôn ḥerpâ*	and with dishonor, reproach.

The repetition of the verbal root *bô'* (x) strengthens the idea that the *rāšā'* (y) and *bûz* (z) go together and provide the major sound patterning in the proverb. It is reinforced by /b/ and sibilant consonance in the same colon.

a. *bbw' rš b' gm bwz*
   bb   š b   b z

The /b/ consonance reinforces the repetition of the verbal root *bô'*, while the sibilants join by sound what the saying joins by meaning: *rāšā'* and *bûz*. The word repetition is clearly enhanced by the additional sound patterning in that colon.

One problem arises in that most commentators change *rāšā'* to *reša'* thus matching the other impersonal terms—*bûz, qālôn* and *ḥerpâ*.[2] But the MT form is quite acceptable since the impersonal terms are qualities adhering in a person and are the *result* of wickedness. The way to understand the proverb would be to see it as building disaster upon disaster with the arrival of the *rāšā'*: *bûz* followed by *qālôn*, followed by *ḥerpâ*, thus:

Cause	Result
bbw' rš'	*b' gm bwz w'm qlwn ḥrph*
(x + y)	(x + z_1 + z_2 + z_3)

1. On this and other proverbs using the word pair *tm* // *'qš*, see W. Brueggemann, 'A Neglected Sapiential Word Pair', *ZAW* 89 (1977), pp. 234-58.

2. Toy, *A Critical Commentary*, p. 355; Scott, *Proverbs*, p. 112; Gemser, *Sprüche*, p. 75; Ringgren, *Sprüche*, p. 74; and McKane, *Proverbs*, p. 521. Barucq (*Le livre*, p. 150) and Delitzsch (*Biblical Commentary*, VI.2, p. 2), on the other hand, follow the MT. The LXX also reads *rāšā'*.

The next series of proverbs to be considered exemplifies intercola repetition. Such repetition is particularly frequent in antithetic or synonymous proverbs. The use of the device in sayings of this type can highlight the tension or contrast of ideas as in the antithetic proverb; it can also emphasize continuity in the development or nuancing of a thought from colon to colon, as in the synonymous proverb. Mere repetition without such variety would be dull; but significant variations in connection with the repetitive pattern create interest. The first group to be analysed, the largest, is composed of antithetic proverbs; then examples of synonymous proverbs will be studied.

Proverbs 10.5. Word repetition and the sound pattern reinforce the sharp antitheses of the portraits in this proverb.

a.	*'ōgēr baqqayiṣ bēn maśkîl*	He who gathers in the summer is a wise son,
b.	*nirdām baqqāṣîr bēn mēbîš*	but he who falls asleep at the harvest is a shameful son.

Again it is *bēn* that is repeated in this proverb and each time it is given an important place in the colon (at the end) with a contrasting adjective immediately attached. In fact, contrast and synonymity play important roles in the structure of this proverb. Between the two cola there is perfect grammatical parallelism. In each case, the parallels on the semantic level are either contrasting or synonymous; but in each case, also, they echo on the level of sound.

semantic:	opposition	equivalence	equivalence	opposition
a.	*'gr*	*baqqayiṣ*	*bēn*	*mśkîl*
b.	*nrdm*	*baqqāṣîr*	*bēn*	*mbîš*
phonic:	repetition	repetition	repetition	repetition
	/r/	/baqq ṣ/	/bēn/	/m, (ś, š), î/

Thus, the grammatical parallelism, the semantic parallelism between the two middle terms of each colon, the word repetition, and the sound patterning all form the background of sameness which serves to emphasize the semantic contrast of the two outside terms of each colon.

Proverbs 13.4. Sound patterns as well as word repetitions play an important role in this antithetic proverb.

a.	*mit'awwâ wā'ayin napšô 'āṣēl*	The lazy person's appetite craves, but in vain;
b.	*wᵉnepeš ḥārūṣîm tᵉduššān*	but the appetite of the diligent is well satisfied.

The repetition of *npš* in each colon next to the contrasting terms *'āṣēl* and *ḥārūṣîm* highlights the tension around which the saying is built. But this is an extremely interesting instance of the phenomenon because it shows the influence that striving after sound patterning can have on normal syntax. Note the unusual construction in the first colon: the subject *npšw* is separated from its predicate *mt'wh* by the nominal sentence *w'yn*. The first colon is to be parsed: participle serving as predicate (*mt'wh*) + intrusive nominal sentence (*w'yn*) + subject (*npš*) + pronoun suffix (*w*) + noun in apposition to the pronoun suffix (*'ṣl*). Two things are unusual about the syntax, the intrusive nominal sentence and the construction *npšw 'ṣl*.

The intrusive nominal sentence will be discussed first. What the proverb-maker has done in the first colon is to place like-sounding words together, specifically, the alliterative motif /'awwâ wā'a/ in *mt'wh w'yn*.[1] Overriding normal syntactical order in the colon is the poet's interest in sound patterning. The MT is quite correct as it is, and attempts to apply 'normal' grammar to a text like this one can only lead to the wrong conclusions. Furthermore, the juxtaposition of the two words pinpoints the thematic antithesis of the colon: 'craving, but no satisfaction'.

As for the construction *npšw 'ṣl*, while it has clear Aramaic connections, it is rarely attested in Hebrew. Thus, *BHK* and *BHS* suggest turning the colon into normal Hebrew either by dropping *npšw* altogether or by deleting the suffix on *npšw*.[2] Because of the word repetition, however, *npš* must obviously remain. More than that, the full phrase *npšw 'ṣl*, with *napšô* as the subject of *mt 'wh* and *'ṣl* defining the suffix on *napšô*, can, perhaps, be defended. The construction is like the phrase *bb'w h'yš* in Ezek. 10.3, *mwty 'ny* in

1. J.J. Glück ('The Figure of "Inversion" in the Book of Proverbs', *Semitics* 5 [1977], p. 30) calls this a case of 'inversion', the suspension of rules of syntax for the sake, in this case, of emphasis.

2. The *BHK* note on *npšw*: 'frt dl (cf GSV) et 1 antea *mit'awweh* nisi mavis *npš* cf T'. *BHS* has fundamentally the same note.

2 Sam. 19.1 and *lnḥštm kl hklym* in Jer. 52.20.[1] The phrase from Prov. 14.13b is particularly appropriate here: *w'ḥryth śmḥh twgh*, 'the end of joy may be sorrow'. The pronoun suffix on *'ḥryth*, defined by appositional *śmḥh*, is employed to obtain the /a/ rhyme throughout the colon. In this case, too, sound patterning could be a consideration. If it can be presumed that the pronunciation of *npš* in the second colon was closer to *napš* than to *nepeš*, that would yield an /a, ā, ū/ phonic sequence in *napš ḥārūṣîm*. This is matched by the /a, ô, a/ sequence in *napšô 'āṣēl*. In addition, the repetition of *npš* from near the end of one colon to the beginning of the next provides the same background in both cola against which the semantic contrast of *'ṣl* and *ḥrṣym* can stand out. For a variety of reasons, therefore, the construction *npšw 'ṣl* can remain as it is.

There are a number of sound patterns in the proverb, mostly linking patterns. Besides the /a, ā, ū, a, ô, a/ sequence just mentioned, there is also a consonant motif involving laryngeals and liquids /(', ḥ), ā, (r, l) ṣ/ which joins *'ṣl* and *ḥrṣym*.[2]

a. *mit'awwâ wā'ayin napšô 'āṣēl*	b. *wᵉnapš* ḥārūṣîm tdšn*
'awwâ wā'a	
a ô ā	*a ā ū*
n pš 'āṣ l	*n pš ḥār ṣ*
n n š ṣ	*n š ṣ m šn*

The final pattern is a motif of nasals and sibilants stretching from *w'yn* to the end of the proverb. Within this group, the connection between the repeated word *npš* and the final verb *tdšn* is emphasized by a /n, š/ sequence which is chiastically reversed in the verb.

1. Joüon, *Grammaire*, §146.e; GKC, §131.n; König, *Historisch-comparative Syntax*, II.2, §284.a. It might be possible to parse *'ṣl* as an adjective, but, in view of nominal *ḥrṣym*, that is less probable.

2. That /'/ and /ḥ/ were close as voiced /h/ and unvoiced /'/ equivalents is clear; e.g., the K. reading *ḥṣ* and the Q. reading *'ṣ* in 1 Sam. 17.7; see *HALAT*, p. 273.

Proverbs 20.6.

a.	*rob 'ādām yiqrā' 'îš ḥasdô*	Many a man proclaims, each one, his own virtue;[1]
b.	*w^{e}'îš '^{e}mûnîm mî yimṣā'*	but who can find a man of trust?

Word repetition is achieved in this proverb by the insertion of *'îš* into the first colon, where strictly speaking it is unnecessary, so as to parallel the *'îš* phrase of the second colon. Its use in the first colon, though practically otiose, is semantically fitting. The juxtaposition of *'îš* with *ḥasdô* emphasizes the self-centeredness of the proclaimed virtue. The repetition of *'îš* emphasizes the contrast between the individual who is in fact a true friend and the many (*rob*) who just say they are.

There is a chiastically structured tagging sound pattern which reinforces the thematic contrast.

a. *rb 'dm yiqrā' 'îš ḥsdw*
yi ā' 'îš
m

b. *w'îš 'mwnîm mî yimṣā'*
'îš yi ā
m m m m
îm mî

One leg of the chiasmus is the repetition of *'îš*. The other leg is founded on the verb in each colon: *yiqrā'*, which expresses the readiness of many to praise themselves, and *yimṣā'*, which alludes to the scarcity of genuine virtue. There is also a /m/ consonance involving *'dm* and the phrase *'mwnym my ymṣ'*. Another sound pattern joins the /m/ consonance to the repetition of the /î/ vowel in the second colon. The first colon is united around a /r, d/ sequence:

a. *rb 'dm yqr' 'yš ḥsdw*
r d r d

To a lesser degree the whole proverb is united around sibilant consonance:

a. . . . *'yš ḥsdw*
š s

b. *w'yš 'mwnym my ymṣ'*
š ṣ

1. So read the RSV; McKane, *Proverbs*, p. 241; Barucq, *Le livre*, p. 158; Gemser, *Sprüche*, p. 78. *BHK* suggests reading *yqr'* as *niphal* with the suffix on *ḥsdw* dropped. *BHS* suggests the adjective *ḥāsîd* rather than *ḥesed*. Toy (*A Critical Commentary*, p. 387) suggests that the suffix is a dittography of the /w/ which begins the second colon.

All these patterns illustrate how sound, structure and sense can work together in a proverb.

Proverbs 28.19. The semantic contrast in this proverb is set against a background of grammatical parallelism and word repetition.

a.	*ʿōbēd ʾadmātô yiśbaʿ lāḥem*	Whoever works his land has his fill of food,
b.	*ûmᵉraddēp rēqîm yiśbaʿ rîš*	but whoever chases after worthless things has his fill of poverty.

The repetition of the verb *yśbʿ* is clearly intended to hammer home the contrast between enough to eat and the lack thereof. The influence of this repetition on meaning is even more manifest when this proverb is contrasted with its near twin, 12.11. The latter saying, dropping the second *yśbʿ*, only changes the last two words, but the change is significant:

a.	*ʿōbēd ʾadmātô yiśbaʿ lāḥem*	Whoever works his land has his fill of food,
b.	*ûmᵉraddēp rēqîm ḥᵃsar lēb*	but whoever chases after worthless things *lacks sense.*

The new wording in the second colon transfers the emphasis from food to characterization of the individuals involved. In Prov. 28.19, on the other hand, the word repetition concentrates on the irony and paradox of the contrast, since 'poverty' can fill nothing. The full effect of this paradox is likewise lost in 28.19b if the ordinary phrase *lʾ yśbʿ* is substituted for *yśbʿ ryš*, even though both phrases have the same meaning.

In addition to the repetition of the sounds in *yśbʿ*, there are other sound patterns throughout the proverb. First of all, the semantic parallelism is largely reflected by sounds. The subject phrase of each colon is composed of different arrangements of the sequence /(b, p), d, m/; the verb, of course, is repeated. The only two words which do not fit into this pattern are the antithetical objects, *lḥm* and *ryš* (whereas in 12.11 *lḥm* and *ḥst lb* share /l/ and /ḥ/).

a.	*ʿbd ʾdmtw yśbʿ lḥm*	b.	*wmrdp rqym yśbʿ ryš*
	bd dm yśbʿ		*m dp m yśbʿ*

Then, there are linking sound patterns as well:

a. *'ōbd 'dmtô yśb' lḥm*	b. *wmrdp rqîm yśb' rîš*
ō d d tô	
' b b'	*b'*
m m	*m m*
	r î rî
	ś š

The resulting picture is that of a network of intricately interwoven sound patterns which tie the whole together.

Proverbs 10.1. The first of the biblical proverbs is the last example of word repetition among the antithetic proverbs to be analysed here. It demonstrates the continuity–tension pattern of the antithetic type well.

a.	*bēn ḥākām y*^{e}*śammaḥ 'āb*	A wise son makes his father glad,
b.	*ûbēn k*^{e}*sîl tûgat 'immô*	but a foolish son is his mother's grief.

The initial position of the repeating word *bēn* in each colon and the fact that, in each case, it is immediately followed (modified) by antithetic ideas calls attention to the tension and opposition being described. The similarities serve to accentuate the differences.

a. *bēn ḥākām y*^{e}*śammaḥ 'āb*	b. *ûbēn k*^{e}*sîl tûgat 'immô*
bēn k ś	*bēn k s*

The proverb loses its impact if the second colon had read *ûk*^{e}*sîl tûgat 'immô* or even *w*^{e}*'îš k*^{e}*sîl tûgat 'immô*.

The relationships between parents and son are also stressed by the sounds of the proverb. A tagging sound pattern, /b, ḥ, m/, distinguishes the subject and the predicate in the first colon but also associates the 'father' and 'wise son' chiastically:

a. *bn ḥkm yśmḥ 'b*
b ḥ m mḥ b

This strong pattern underlines the happy relationship involved. The second colon has a more limited sound pattern, /(n, m), (k, g)/, which reflects the semantic coordination in that colon.

b. *wbn ksyl twgt 'mw*
n k g m

The weakness of the euphony would also be an apt phonic representation of the strained relations involved. One final note: 'father' and 'mother', though divided between the cola, are to be understood together in each colon. Thus, the wise son brings joy to his father and mother, and the foolish one brings grief to both.

Proverbs 17.6. This is the first example of word repetition among the synonymous proverbs.

a.	*ʿᵃṭeret zᵉqēnîm bᵉnê bānîm*	The crown of old men is grandchildren
b.	*wᵉtip'eret bānîm 'ᵃbôtām*	and the glory of children is their parentage.

The saying revolves around the complementary relations associated with the repetition of *bānîm*—children as regards their elders and elders as regards their children. The close association portrayed between these people is reflected, as well, by the sound patterns. The words for children are related by a /b, n, îm/ motif which is echoed by the /b, m/ sounds in *'ᵃbôtām*, 'the parents', and the /nîm/ sequence in *zᵉqēnîm*, 'their elders'. The first words in each colon are related by the alliteration of /(ṭ, t), eret/.

a.	*ʿᵃṭeret zᵉqēnîm bᵉnê bānîm*	b.	*wᵉtip'eret banîm 'ᵃbôtām*
	nîm b n b nîm		*b nîm b m*
	ṭeret		*t eret*
	(ṭart)		*(art)*

This is in addition to the sound repetition involved in the two occurrences of *bānîm* and the labial consonance /(b, p)/ throughout most of the proverb.

The sound pattern relating *ʿᵃṭeret* and *tip'eret*, furthermore, is significant because it joins two words, normally linked together in a stereotyped phrase (as in Prov. 4.9; 16.31; Isa. 62.3; Jer. 13.18; Ezek. 16.12; and 23.42), but now separated in order to introduce each colon of the proverb. The combination *ʿṭrt tp'rt*, like *šd wšbr* (Isa. 59.7; 60.18) and *šmyr wšyt* (Isa. 5.6; 7.23, 24, 25; 9.17), was created, first of all, because of the striking consonance of the combination and retained that way in the tradition for the same reason. The same factors led to the creation of 'kith and kin' in English, and tradition has preserved the word 'kith' only in this combination. Although the combination was broken up in order to introduce each colon, the proverb maker surely intended the whole expression to be understood in the use of each word of the expression.[1] Thus, the intended sense for the proverb is, 'Children and their ancestors are each other's glorious crown'. A semantic chiasmus in the saying brings like terms together:

a. . . . *z^e^qēnîm b^e^nê bānîm*
(old) (young)
b. . . . *bānîm 'ᵃbôtām*
(young) (old)

Proverbs 27.8. Word repetition in this proverb forms the background for a simile.

a. *k^e^ṣippôr nôdedet min qinnāh*	Like a bird wandering far from its nest,
b. *kēn 'îš nôdēd mimm^e^qômô*	so a man wandering far from his home.

The cola, related as predicate and subject, manifest partial grammatical and semantic parallelism. The sound patterns are built on a nearly identical pattern:

a. *kṣpôr nôdedet mn qhn*	b. *kn 'yš nôdēd mmqômô*
kṣ ô nôded mn q n	*kn š nôdēd mmqômô*

Thus, the sound pattern in each colon tags each part of the simile. The nasals /n, m/ and the repeating long /o/ vowels of each colon keep

1. For a study of this phenomenon, see E.Z. Melamed, 'Break up of Stereotype Phrases as an Artistic Device in Biblical Poetry', *Scripta Hierosolymitana* 8 (1961), pp. 115-53. Zech. 9.10 is another good example:

whkrty rkb m'prym
wsws myrwšlm

This verse surely does not mean that only chariots will be banished from Ephraim and only horses from Jerusalem! Jerusalem and Ephraim represent the whole of God's people (Israel and Judah). The phrase *sws wrkb* is a common enough one (Josh. 11.4, etc.) for the horse-drawn chariot. Although the phrase was broken up for the sake of parallelism, the verse is understood to refer to the removal of all horse-drawn chariots from both Jerusalem and Ephraim. Also, note how the break-up in Zech. 9.10 contributes to the sound pattern:

whkrty rkb m'prym
kr rk
r b pr
wsûs myrûšlm
sûs ûš

echoing the initial sound of the repeated key word *ndd*.

Worth noting too is the contrast between the contracted and uncontracted forms of the preposition *min*, which complement the euphony of the whole saying. The first use, the uncontracted *min*, is chosen to echo /n/ of *nddt* and *qnh* of its own colon, and the /n/ of *kn* and *ndd* in the second colon. The second *min*, however, is contracted in order to echo the /m/ sounds in the final word *mqwm*. The standard English pronunciation of the 'three Rs'—'reading, (w)riting and (a)rithmetic'—presents a similar example of the influence of sound patterning on morphology. The semantic, syntactic and phonic parallelisms reinforce the simile, especially the equivalence of the *'yš* and the *špwr*, the only words in the parallel cola with a marked semantic difference. The relationship between those two words is the point the proverb wants to make. There is, finally, a semantic-sonant chiasmus in the proverb. The words *nôdedet* and *nôdēd* form the semantic half, while a /(k, q), n/ motif joins *qnh* and *kn* in the sonant link.

a.	. . . *nôdedet* . . .	*qnh*	b.	*kn* . . .	*nôdēd* . . .
	nôdedet	*qn*		*kn*	*nôdēd*

Proverbs 21.30. A triple repetition is the backbone of this proverb.

a.	*'ên ḥokmâ* w^{e}*'ên* t^{e}*bûnâ*	There is no wisdom and no understanding
b.	w^{e}*'ên 'ēṣâ* l^{e}*neged* YHWH	and no counsel when facing the Lord.

The triple repetition of anaphoric *'ên* followed in each case by a synonym ending in /â/ forms an emphatic negation, the background of sameness that isolates and emphasizes the final climax *lngd* YHWH. Apart from this, there is also a strong consonance in /n/.

a.	*'ên*	*ḥkmâ*	w^{e}*'ên*	*tbwnâ*	b.	w^{e}*'ên*	*'ṣâ*	*lngd* YHWH
	'ên	*â*	*'ên*	*â*		*'ên*	*â*	*n*

The repetition of words and sounds in this proverb actually presents a sense of climax which can be graphically represented as follows:

a. *'ên ḥokmâ*
w^{e}*'ên* t^{e}*bûnâ*
b. w^{e}*'ên 'ēṣâ* l^{e}*neged* YHWH

The words *lngd* YHWH, concluding the final *'ên* clause, stop this climactic thrust with the culminating idea toward which the repetition has been leading. The final colon actually says everything necessary, but hardly as well without the emphatic negations of the first colon.

Proverbs 21.17. This proverb is another example of that type of proverb, discussed in the previous chapter, where the structure of the proverb shifts in the fourth element.[1]

a.	*'îš maḥsôr 'ōhēb śimḥâ*	A poor man is a lover of pleasure;
b.	*'ōhēb yayin wāšemen lō' ya'ᵃšîr*	a lover of wine and oil will not grow rich.

The first colon is a nominal sentence composed of two phrases (*'îš maḥsôr* and *'ōhēb śimḥâ*), each of which combines a substantive (*'îš*, a noun, and *'ōhēb*, a participle) with a dependent genitive (*maḥsôr* and *śimḥâ*). The association of the two phrases is dramatically paralleled in the phonic pattern of the colon:

a.	*'îš maḥsôr*	*'ōhēb śimḥâ*
	š m ḥsô	*ō ś mḥ*

The second colon begins in a similar fashion with a phrase which repeats *'ōhēb* and combines it with *two* nouns in the construct, *yayin wāšemen*, a small variation in the pattern. But then the pattern changes completely. The addition of the final verbal element, *lō' ya'ᵃšîr*, turns the second colon into a verbal sentence. The move from a nominal to a verbal sentence not only marks the conclusion of the proverb but also adds emphasis to the final statement of the theme. A tagging sound pattern marks subject and predicate in this colon.

b.	*'ōhb yyn wšmn*	*lō' y'šyr*
	ō yy š	*ō y š*

It is worth noting at this point how the prefix tense of the verb fits here because its /y/ picks up *yyn*. That *ma'asir* or *'asir* would not be effective in this way is patent. Even switching the positions of the phrases *'hb śmḥh* and *'hb yyn wšmn*, though making no semantic difference at all, would significantly weaken the sound patterns outlined above.

There is more. The sound patterns connecting the two *'ōhēb* phrases (the subjects in their respective clauses) echo the semantic connection between those phrases.

a.	*. . . 'ōhēb śmḥh*	b.	*'ōhēb yyn wšmn . . .*
	'ōhēb śm		*'ōhēb šm*

1. See Prov. 20.19, Chapter 6.

The repetition offers phonic and semantic continuity between the simple statement of the first colon and the more emphatic statement contained in the second colon. The echoing effect involving the repetition of *'hb* and these other sounds indicates on the level of sound that the *'hb śmḥh* is defined by *'hb yyn wšmn*. What is really being talked about is the *'hb śmḥt yyn wšmn*. The two predicates are also related phonically by the sibilants /š, s/, /r/, and the two gutturals /', ḥ/.[1]

a.	*'yš mḥswr . . .*	b. *. . . l' y'šyr*
	š ḥs r	*š r*

The full sense, then, of the proverb is plain: the pleasures loved are wine and oil, and the expense involved in enjoying these does not allow one to grow rich. The word repetition, semantic structure, and the phonic pattern in the proverb, therefore, emphasize the grammatical chiasmus connecting the parallel phrases:

a.	*'îš maḥsôr*	*'ōhēb śimḥâ*
	Pred.	Subj.
b.	*'ōhēb yayin wāšemen*	*lō' ya'ašîr*
	Subj.	Pred.

The chiasmus emphasizes the paradox of the whole saying: living like a king and being poor go together!

Proverbs 22.29.

a.	*ḥāzîtā 'îš māhîr bimᵉla'ktô*	Do you see a man skilled at his work?
b.	*lipnê mᵉlākîm yityaṣṣāb*	He shall stand up before kings;
c.	*bal yityaṣṣēb lipnê ḥᵃšukkîm*	he shall not stand forth before unknowns.

The word repetition in this proverb involves the preposition *lpny* and the verb *ytyṣb*. The common background created by the repetition of *lpny. . . ytyṣb* (colon b) and *bl ytyṣb lpny* (colon c) calls attention to the contrast between *mlkym* and *ḥškym*. It is this contrast that makes the fundamental point of the proverb. A chiastic arrangement is thus achieved with the two cola:

b.	*lpny mlkym*	*ytyṣb*
	A	B
c.	*bl ytyṣb*	*lpny ḥškym*
	B′	A′

1. /'/ and /ḥ/ are phonically related, as pointed out in a previous note.

The chiasmus links those cola closely together and highlights the contrast.

Naturally enough, strong sound patterns echo this chiasmus. Besides the sounds involved in the repetition of *lpny* and *ytyṣb*, there is also the rhyming alliteration of /kîm/ on *m^{e}lākîm* and *ḥ^{a}šukkîm* to add to the pattern. The result is a phonic chiasmus built on a tagging sound pattern.

a.	*lipnê m^{e}lākîm*	*yityaṣṣāb*
	lipnê kîm	*yityaṣṣāb*
b.	*bl yityaṣṣēb*	*lipnê ḥ^{a}šukkîm*
	yityaṣṣēb	*lipnê kkîm*

On the semantic and phonic levels the structures of these two cola coincide.

Colon a has the purpose of preparing for the assertions in colons b and c and even invites the hearer's response, 'Do you see. . .?' On the level of sound this colon has a strong assonance in long /i/ vowels. It also shares some consonance with the other two cola. The first word *ḥzyt* shares a /ḥ, (z, š)/ sequence with the last word of the saying, *ḥškym*. There is also a /m, l, k/ motif shared by *bml'ktw* of the first colon and *mlkym* of the second.[1]

a.	*ḥzît 'îš mhîr bml'ktw*	b.	*lpny mlkym ytyṣb*	c.	*bl ytyṣb lpny ḥškym*
	ḥz ml k		*mlk*		*ḥš*

Against the background of all these semantic and phonic relationships in the proverb it becomes more difficult to accept the view of a number of critics that the third colon is an addition. The basic problem seems to be that the triplet format is relatively rare in Proverbs. So the offending third colon is either bracketed,[2] or it is assumed to be the last half of another saying whose first colon is missing.[3] Recourse is had to the similar themes in Sir. 8.8, 38.3 and 39.4 as justification for separating the third colon from the rest of the saying.[4] Another source of comparison is *Amen-em-opet* 27.16-17:

1. Boström, *Paronomasi*, p. 193.
2. Ringgren, *Sprüche*, p. 89 n. 4; Scott, *Proverbs*, p. 138.
3. Gemser, *Sprüche*, p. 84.
4. Gemser, *Sprüche*, p. 84.

As for the scribe who is experienced in his office,
He will find himself worthy (to be) a courtier.[1]

But the absence of an antithetic response to the second colon in the comparative material does not preclude its presence in Proverbs. Nor do the biblical sayings need to be exact copies of Egyptian ones. If the word repetition and phonic structures of this proverb show anything, it is that the third colon, whether an addition or not, has been carefully integrated with the other two cola

Proverbs 11.7. The repetition of the different forms of the verb *'bd* sounds the keynote for this proverb.

a.	*b^{e}môt 'ādām rāšā' tō'bad tiqwâ*	When a wicked person dies, hope perishes;
b.	*w^{e}tôḥelet 'ônîm 'ābạdâ*	and trust placed in wealth is destroyed.

The basic theme of the proverb seems to be that when the person dies, whatever hope or reliance was placed on the things that life and strength could offer dies as well. In modern terms the proverb is saying, 'You can't take it with you'. The proverb actually goes one step further and specifies the individual mentioned (and presumably his 'hope') as *rš'*.

Clear sound patterns connect these cola. Throughout the proverb there is the consonance /b, (d, t)/.

a.	*bmwt*	*'dm*	*rš'*	*t'bd*	*tqwh*
	b t	*d*		*t bd*	*t*

b.	*wtwḥlt*	*'wnym*	*'bdh*
	t t		*bd*

Only one word in each colon is not affected by this consonance, *rš'* in the first and *'wnym* in the second. In addition, the /t/ series, which links the phrase *tō'bad tiqwâ* at the end of the first colon, is carried on by the first word of the next colon, *tôḥelet*, and is reinforced by a long /o/ assonance that accompanies each occurrence of /t/ in the proverb except for *tiqwâ*. The /o/ vowel series is repeated for the last time in *'ônîm*.

a.	*b^{e}môt*	*'ādām*	*rāšā'*	*tō'bad*	*tiqwâ*
				t	*t*
	ôt			*tō*	

b.	*w^{e}tôḥelet*	*'ônîm*	*'ābādâ*
	t t		
	tô	*ô*	

Even the repeated verb forms come into play. The *t*-prefix verb form in the first colon shares a /t/ consonance with its subject *tqwh*, as

1. *ANET*, p. 424.

explained above. The form of the same verb in the second colon is determined at least in part by the desire to create an end rhyme with *tiqwâ*.

a. . . . *t'bd tiqwâ* b. . . . *'ābādâ*
t t
â â

This would partially explain the *tqṭl–qṭl* verb sequence in the proverb.[1] All told, the proverb is a well-knit whole on the level of sound.

A difficulty raised with respect to this proverb is the unusual length of the first colon. It has been suggested that the deletion of *'dm* would shorten the colon but not affect the sense.[2] However, from the point of view of the sound patterns *'dm* belongs to the proverb and probably ought not to be dropped. On the other hand, the only word unaffected by the sound patterns is *rš'* and at least on this level could be eliminated without any problem. The presence of *rš'* in the proverb is defended by an appeal to *'ônîm* in the second colon. It is felt by some translators that the word in one way or another ought to mean 'evil men' and parallel *rš'*.[3] But *'ônîm* (not from *'āwen*, which is otherwise not used in the plural) is the plural intensive form for *'ôn*, 'vigor, wealth', and it is very questionable whether the word ever meant 'evil'.[4] The full phrase *twḥlt 'wnym* ('trust placed in wealth') fits neatly into the theme of the proverb with *rš'* omitted. *Twḥlt 'wnym* is a refinement, a clarification of *tqwh* in the previous colon and complements the contrast between death and the futile hopes placed on wealth. Even on the semantic level, then, *rš'* could be deleted.

The word *rāšā'* could possibly be a later addition to the proverb when it was felt that the tone of the proverb was too irreverent or

1. M. Held, 'The *YQTL–QTL (QTL–YQTL)* Sequence of Identical Verbs in Biblical Hebrew and in Ugaritic', in *Studies and Essays in Honor of Abraham A. Neuman* (ed. M. Ben-Horin, B.D. Weinryb and S. Zeitlin; Leiden: Brill, 1962), pp. 281-90.

2. Gemser, *Sprüche*, p. 54; Ringgren, *Sprüche*, p. 48; Toy, *A Critical Commentary*, p. 225.

3. LXX, RSV have 'godless'; Toy, *A Critical Commentary*, pp. 223, 225; W.O.E. Oesterley, *The Book of Proverbs* (New York: E.P. Dutton, 1929), p. 83; Held, 'The *YQTL–QTL* Sequence', p. 281.

4. Delitzsch, *Biblical Commentary*, VI.1, p. 233.

pessimistic as it was and had to be brought into line with religious thought. In fact, the LXX translates this proverb by constructing an antithesis in which the eternal (beyond the grave) hope of the just man is contrasted with the boasting (καύχημα) of the wicked, which is destroyed.[1] The justification, however, for the LXX's changes are not clear: an erroneous reading of *yāšār* for *rāšā'*? A faulty Hebrew text before the Greek translators?[2] An accommodation of the text to a nascent belief in an afterlife—at least for the just?

The context in which Prov. 11.7 finds itself is another important consideration. It is surrounded by other sayings whose theme is: the just survive, the wicked perish (see, for instance, Prov. 11.6 and 8). Whether or not 11.7 had *rš'* originally, the editor would have had the destruction of the wicked in mind when placing the proverb here. Adding *rš'* would simply accommodate the proverb to the context. Originally, however, independent of this context, the proverb would have simply meant: at death the hope of all (good and wicked) perishes (Eccl. 3.19-20; 9.2-5; Job 21.23-26; Ps. 49.12, 20). The presence of *'ônîm* in the second colon could also have attracted *rš'* to the proverb. 'Wealth' (*'wn*) is associated with the 'wicked' (*rš'*) in Job 20.10 and with the 'sinner' in Hos. 12.9. A long-standing tradition in the OT connects the wicked with wealth (Amos 4.1; 5.11-12; 6.4-7; 8.6; Mic. 6.12; Job 27.16-17; Prov. 13.22) in contrast to the 'righteous poor'. The use of *rš'* in the first colon would produce a natural parallelism in the proverb: *rš'* // *'ônîm*. All in all, it is clear that if anything is to be deleted as secondary, a case can be made for regarding *rš'* as the plus; *'dm* cannot easily be regarded as such.

Proverbs 24.29. This is the last proverb to be considered that involves word repetition. Some follow the MT division of this proverb. This leads to an unusually long first colon. This problem can be resolved by regarding the proverb as a quatrain with the first colon introducing the quotation that appears in the other three cola. For the convenience of this analysis, the quatrain structure will be used. The quotation itself, contained within the proverb, demonstrates a reciprocal use of the intercola repetition of verbs. To put it simply, the subject of the verb, when first used, becomes the object of the verb when it is

1. Delitzsch, *Biblical Commentary*, VI.1, p. 233.; Barucq, *Le livre*, p. 108.
2. Barucq, *Le livre*, p. 108.

repeated. The theme of the quotation, retaliation, is aptly highlighted by this reciprocal association of the identical verbs.

a.	*'al tō'mar*	Don't say,
b.	*ka'*^{a}*šer 'āśâ lî*	'As he did to me,
c.	*kēn 'e'*^{e}*śeh lô*	thus I'll do to him;
d.	*'āšîb lā'îš k*^{e}*po'*^{o}*lô*	I'll repay the man according to his deed!'

The reciprocity of retaliation is expressed by the two verbs, *'āśâ* and *'e'*^{e}*śeh*, found in cola b and c. The repetition of the verb is qualified in each case so that the first occurrence, *'āśâ*, is third person with a first person indirect object, *lî*, expressing completed action; the second usage, *'e'*^{e}*śeh*, is first person with a third person indirect object, *lô*, with the sense of an action intended. Subjects and objects, as well as the quality of the verbal action, have been switched from one colon to the next aptly underscoring the quotation within the proverb. The repetition of the same verbal root highlights the underlying motive: retaliation.

This relationship is emphasized by the sound patterns used in the cola in which the verbs occur. A tagging sound pattern, /k, (š, ś), ', l/, marks each of the cola highlighting the semantic reciprocity.

b.	*k'šr 'śh ly*	c.	*kn ''śh lw*
	k š 'ś l		*k 'ś l*

The last colon, which restates the sentiment of colon c, also picks up this same phonic pattern:

d.	*'šyb l'yš kp'lw*
	š l š k 'l

An assonance in /a/ vowels marks the first two cola (a and b):

a.	*'al tō'mar*	b.	*ka'*^{a}*šer 'āśâ lî*
	a a		*a ā â*

The last colon has both long /î/ and /ô/ vowels, which pick up sounds in cola b and c. The /î/ vowel first occurs in *lî* at the end of colon b. The /î/ vowel occurs again in colon d in the verb *'āšîb* and its object *la'îš*. The /ô/ vowel appears at the end of colon c in *lô*, and again in the last colon in *k*^{e}*po'*^{o}*lô*. Another sequence of sounds between colon c and d, /k, ', lô/, completes the phonic picture.

b.	*. . . lî*	c.	*kn ''śh lô*	d.	*'āšîb lā'îš k*^{e}*po'*^{o}*lô*
			k ' lô		*k ' lô*
	lî				*î l î*

Although this proverb is long and seemingly unbalanced, there can be little doubt, at least from the point of view of sound, that it all belongs together. In the light of such sound patterning, the suggestion of *BHS* to add *gam 'ānî* after *'eʿeśeh lô* 'for the sake of meter' is very questionable since the new phrase would be an extraneous element that echoes in only a minimum fashion the sound patterns typical of the proverb.

2. *Repetition of Word Roots*

Introduction

In this section it is not the same individual words that are repeated, but words derived from the same root. This means, therefore, that the repetition normally involves a noun (or adjective) and a verb (or participle). Such root repetition, just like word repetition, necessarily involves the repetition of various sounds as well and so is logically included here.

Texts

Proverbs 17.15. The effect of the double repetition in the first colon is derived from the way it combines the opposed notions of 'declaring the guilty innocent' and 'the innocent guilty' in chiastic order.

a.	*maṣdîq rāšāʿ ûmaršîaʿ ṣaddîq*	Whoever condones the wicked and whoever condemns the just
b.	*tôʿabat YHWH gam šenêhem*	are both an abomination to the Lord.

The repeating roots, each represented by a participle and an adjective (*maṣdîq* and *ṣaddîq*; *maršîaʿ* and *rāšāʿ*), are strategically located in a chiastic pattern: the *ršʿ* root words in the middle of the colon next to each other and the *ṣdq* root words at either end of the colon. Each participle also has the same format, /ma + î/, which contributes to the sound patterning.

	participle +	object +	participle +	object
a.	*maṣdîq*	*rāšāʿ*	*ûmaršîaʿ*	*ṣaddîq*
	ma î		*ma î*	
	ṣd q			*ṣ dd q*
		r š ʿ	*rš ʿ*	

Though the two notions are opposed, the point of the proverb is that both are equally condemnable.

This equality is underscored by triple repetition: repetition of grammatical structure (participle + object // participle + object), of word roots (*ṣdq* and *rš‘*), and, therefore, of sound as well. The intertwining of all three types of repetition in the one colon emphasizes on the level of sound the extent to which the two opposing processes are intertwined in reality by reason of their joint condemnation, given by the second colon's judgment: *tw‘bt*. The connection between first and second cola is underscored by the way the /t, ‘/ sequence of *tw‘bt* picks up the /d/ and /‘/ consonance of the first colon, and by *šᵉnêhem*, which echoes the /m/ and sibilant consonance in the first colon.

a. *mṣdyq rš‘ wmršy‘ ṣdyq*   b. *tw‘bt* YHWH *gm šnyhm*
d ‘ ‘ d   *t ‘ t*
mṣ š m š ṣ   *m š m*

Proverbs 15.27. This proverb exemplifies the format previously discussed whereby the structure of the proverb changes in the last phrase.[1]

a. *‘ōkēr bêtô bôṣēa‘ bāṣa‘* One who grabs unjust gain is one who upsets his own house;
b. *wᵉśônē’ mattānōt yiḥyeh* but the one who hates bribes will live.

The first colon is a nominal sentence involving two participles (*‘ōkēr* and *bôṣēa‘*) each with a dependent ‘genitive’ object (*bêtô* and *bāṣa‘*). The coordination of these phrases as subject and predicate is reflected in the sound patterns.

a. *‘ōkēr bêtô bôṣēa‘ bāṣa‘*
b ṣ ‘b ṣ ‘
‘ b b ‘b ‘
ō ē ê ô ô ē

First of all, there is the *figura etymologica* in *bôṣēa‘ bāṣa‘*. Then the /b, ‘/ sequence of *bwṣ‘ bṣ‘* is reflected, reversed, with the first letter of each word in the predicate *‘kr bytw*. In addition, the long /o/ and /e/ pattern of *bôṣēa‘* is also echoed in those same words.

The second colon begins like the first with a participial phrase (*śônē’ mattānōt*). This *qal* participial format with long /o/ and /e/ assonance joins this colon to the sound and forms of the first colon.

1. See Prov. 20.19, Chapter 6.

But the contrasting sense of this colon is given emphasis by the switch from the participle plus object format to the imperfect verbal form *yiḥyeh* at the end of the colon. The syntax highlights the antithesis, therefore, while the sounds of the second colon reflect the previous colon.

b. *w*^{e}*śônē' mattānōt yiḥyeh*
ô e ō eh (< *ay*)

Although *yiḥyeh* ends the participial pattern of the proverb, it still echoes and concludes the vowel sounds of those participles.

Proverbs 14.5. In this saying there are two sets of repetitions involving the word *'ēd*, and the root *kzb*.

a.	*'ēd '*^{e}*mûnîm lō' y*^{e}*kazzēb*	A truthful witness does not lie,
b.	*w*^{e}*yāpîaḥ*[1] *k*^{e}*zābîm 'ēd šāqer*	but a deceitful witness breathes forth lies.

In the first colon the two repeating words are at either end and *ykzb* is a verb; in the second colon they are in the middle and *kzbym* is a noun. Also, their positions relative to each other are reversed from colon to colon, thus forming a chiasmus:

a. *'ēd . . . y*^{e}*kazzēb*
b. . . . *k*^{e}*zābîm 'ēd . . .*

Aside from the sounds involved in the word repetition alone, there are other sound patterns which relate both cola. The first one uses the repeated words plus the ending /îm/ in a sequence that connects both cola. The sequence is reversed from first colon to second.

a. *'ēd 'mwnîm l' ykzb* b. *wypyḥ kzbîm 'ēd šqr*
'ēd îm kzb *kzbîm 'ēd*

This phonic sequence largely reflects the semantic chiasmus. A different sequence of sounds, /y, (k, q), (b, p)/, forms another link beginning with the verb *ykzb*:

a. *'d 'mwnym l' ykzb* b. *wypyḥ kzbym 'd šqr*
yk b *yp k b q*

Proverbs 17.18. In this saying the use of the *figura etymologica* in the second colon establishes clear sound patterns.

1. On *ypyḥ*, see p. 43 n. 2.

a. *'ādām ḥ^a^sar lēb tôqēa' kāp*	A senseless person is the one who gives his hand in a pledge;
b. *'ōrēb '^a^rubbâ lipnê rē'ēhû*	who becomes security in the presence of his neighbor.

The proverb, first of all, is constructed of one predicate (*'dm ḥsr lb*) followed by the two participial phrases acting as subjects. Semantically, the participial terms are parallel (B and B′), with the final prepositional phrase (C) carrying the thought a little further in order to conclude it emphatically: the foolish bargain is even sealed publicly (*lpny r'hw*)!

a. *'dm ḥsr lb*	*twq' kp*
A	B
Pred.	Subj. 1

b. *'rb 'rbh lpny r'hw*
B′ C
Subj. 2

In addition, the notion of 'pledging' is usually conveyed simply by the use of the verb *'rb* alone, as in Prov. 6.1 or 11.15. But here the *figura etymologica* emphasizes the practice being discouraged by the double occurrence of the same root and sets up a phonic motif which picks up sounds only loosely distributed in the first colon. The /', r, (b, p)/ sequence of *'rb 'rbh* is repeated, but reversed, in the last phrase *lpny r'hw*.

a. *'dm ḥsr lb twq' kp*	b. *'rēb 'rbh lpny rē'ēhû*
r b ' p	*'r b 'rb p r '*

Proverbs 16.26. A noun and a verb from the same root are joined in the first colon as part of the subject and the predicate. They not only express the principal idea of the entire proverb, but their repetition dramatically reinforces it on the level of sound.

a. *nepeš 'āmēl 'ām^e^lâ lô*	The worker's appetite works on his behalf,
b. *kî 'ākap 'ālāyw pîhû*	for his mouth urges him on.

The sounds of /', m, l/ are the principal pattern of the first colon, and are echoed by *lô* and, in the second colon, by *'ālāyw*. The use of the preposition in the second colon brings some of the sounds of the key words of the first colon into the second, helping to underscore the synonymity of the cola.

a. *nepeš ʿāmēl ʿāmᵉlâ lô* b. *kî ʾākap ʿālāyw pîhû*
ʿ m l ʿ m l l *ʿ l*

There is another intercola sequence /p, ʿ, l/ that also binds both cola together.

a. *npš ʿml ʿmlh lw* b. *ky ʾkp ʿlyw pyhw*
p ʿ l *p ʿl*

Finally, in the second colon, there is also the repetition of /k/, /i/ and /p/ to bring the cola together phonically.

b. *kî ʾākap ʿālāyw pîhû*
kî k p pî

Proverbs 29.7. The use of the *ydʿ* root at the beginning and again at the end of the saying forms a bracket or frame for the theme.

a.	*yōdēaʿ ṣaddîq dîn dallîm*	The just man shows concern for the cause of the poor;
b.	*rāšāʿ lōʾ yābîn dāʿat*	the wicked man knows no concern.

The proverb focuses on the relation of the just man and the wicked man to 'concern (for the poor)'. It calls attention to this concern by root repetition. The consonants of the root then figure heavily in the sound patterning. There is a /d, î/ sequence, primarily in the first colon, to associate the *ṣaddîq*'s concern (*ydʿ*) with the *dîn dallîm*. The /în, d/ sequence of the phrase *dîn dallîm* of the first colon alliterates with the phrase *yābîn dāʿat* in the second colon underscoring the contrast between the cola. A final phonic motif, based on the consonants of the repeating root /y, d, ʿ/, appears in the last colon. The various phonic patterns look this way:

a. *ydʿ ṣdîq dîn dlîm* b. *ršʿ lʾ ybîn dʿt*
d dî dî d î
în d *în d*
ydʿ *y dʿ*

Proverbs 22.22-23. In the following quatrain, the repetition of words takes on an ironic twist.

22a.	*'al tigzol dāl kî dal hû'*	Don't steal from a poor person because he's poor,
b.	*w^{e}'al t^{e}dakkē' 'ānî baššā'ar*	and don't crush the oppressed at the gate,
23a.	*kî YHWH yārîb rîbām*	for the Lord will plead their plea,
b.	*w^{e}qāba' 'et qōb^{e}'êhem nāpeš*	and rob their robbers of life.

The repetition of the word *dal*, in the first colon of v. 22, underlines the note of cowardice ('because he's poor' and thus easy prey) in the sin of injustice (stealing from the poor). But the repetition of the roots *ryb* and *qb'* in the first and second cola of v. 23 creates an ironic contrast with the first two cola (v. 22) in that these latter repetitions draw attention to how the tables are being turned on the oppressors. In 23a, the Lord himself will take up the plea of those whose plea has gone unheeded, and in the next colon, 23b, the 'robbers' are about to become the 'robbed'—again, because of the Lord.

In the first colon of v. 22 the consonants of the repeated word contribute to a phonic chiasmus, which links that colon to the next, /l, d, (g, k)/:

22a. *'al tgzl dāl ky dal hw'*   b. *w'al tdk' 'ny bš'r*
l g   d l k   d l   *l dk*
al   dāl   dal   *al*

The combination of the /a/ vowel with the /d/ and /l/ creates an alliterative pattern: *al* - *dāl* - *dal* - *al*.[1]

In the first and second cola of v. 23 the word repetitions form the major sound patterns in each case, but there is /î/ assonance in 23a, and *nāpeš* at the end of the second colon is something of an echo of *'ny bš'r* in 22b by reason of the motif /n (b, p), š,/ in each phrase.

22b. . . . *'ny bš'r*
n bš
23a. *kî YHWH yārîb rîbām*
rîb rîb
î   î   î
23b. *wqb' 't qb'yhm npš*
npš
qb'   qb'

Proverbs 24.19-20. This quatrain is constructed on a pattern of two motive clauses answering to two prohibitions. Each prohibition is

1. Boström, *Paronomasi*, p. 193.

linked to its own particular motive clause by word and root repetition.

19a.	*'al tiṯhar bamm^erē'îm*	Don't be provoked by evildoers
b.	*'al t^eqannē' bār^ešā'îm*	nor be envious of the wicked—
20a.	*kî lō' tihyeh 'aḥ^arît lārā'*	for the evil person has no future.
b.	*nēr r^ešā'îm yid'āk*	The lamp of the wicked will be extinguished.

The first prohibition (19a) is joined to its motive clause (20a) by the repetition of the root *r''*. Colon 19a has the participial form *m^erē'îm*, while 20a uses the adjectival form *rā'*. In addition, these two cola are related by the motif /l, t, ḥ, r/ in both *ttḥr* and *'ḥryt*. Both cola also have a /l/ consonance.

19a.	*'l ttḥr bmr'ym*	20a.	*ky l' thyh 'ḥryt lr'*
	r'		*r'*
	l ttḥr		*l t ḥr t l*

The prohibition in 19b is related to its motive clause (20b) by the repetition of the word *r^ešā'îm* in both cola and the consonantal motif /(t, d), (q, k)/ between the verbs *tqn'* and *yd'k*—these patterns being arranged chiastically.

19b.	*'l tqn' brš'ym*	20b.	*nr rš'ym yd'k*
	tq rš'ym		*rš'ym d k*

But the prohibitions (19a and b) and the motive clauses (20a and b) have, in addition, their own distinctive sound patterning. The first two cola are joined by the sequence /'al, t, b, r, 'îm/.

19a.	*'al ttḥr bmr'îm*	19b.	*'al tqn' brš'îm*
	'al t b r'îm		*'al t br 'îm*

The motive clauses (20a and b) have a /k/ consonance to open and close the verse plus two motifs, /t, r/ and /r, '/:

20a.	*ky l' thyh 'ḥryt lr'*	20b.	*nr rš'ym yd'k*
	k		*k*
	t r t r		
	r'		*r r ' '*

3. *Wordplay*

Introduction

This section will deal with the repetition of similar sounding words that have different meanings.[1] Put another way, it involves different words that in whole or in part sound alike. This broad category of wordplay includes different words that can be pronounced alike (homophones), even spelled alike (homonyms), or just be somewhat close in sound (paronomasia). The words 'too' and 'two', 'write' and 'right' are all examples of homophones. Homonyms are represented by such words as 'chase' (either in the sense of 'pursue' or 'decorate metal') and 'pool' (the game or the body of water). But it is the last type, paronomasia, involving words with less similar sounds, which will be illustrated with regard to the proverbs.

Paronomasia is the repetition of words that are somewhat the same in sound.[2] An example is found in what Shakespeare's Falstaff says to Prince Hal, 'were it not here apparent that thou art heir apparent' (*Henry IV Part I,* I.ii.64). The wordplay signals a change in the conversation because Falstaff, after this remark, begins to ask the Prince about what he will do when crowned king. The similarity of sound between 'here' and 'heir' and the repetition of 'apparent' draws attention to itself and has the effect of subtly reminding the listener again of just who this Hal is—or will become. The new drift in the conversation is thereby introduced. One last example of paronomasia, where the sounds are even less similar, is also from Shakespeare:[3] 'Out sword, and to a sore purpose!' (*Cymbeline*, IV.i.25). Such exploitations of similar sounding words are especially useful for drawing out the irony or humor in a situation.

1. M. Joseph, *Shakespeare's Use of the Arts of Language* (New York: Columbia University Press, 1947), p. 164; also, S.F. Fogle, 'Pun', in Preminger (ed.), *Princeton Encyclopedia of Poetry and Poetics*, p. 681.
2. Fogle, 'Pun', p. 681.
3. Fogle, 'Pun', p. 681.

Texts

Proverbs 13.20.

a. *hālôk 'et ḥ^{a}kāmîm waḥ^{a}kām*[1]	Walk with the wise and so become wise;
b. *w^{e}rō'eh k^{e}sîlîm yērôa'*	but a follower of fools will face harm.

Both cola represent a transition from 'being with' to 'becoming': in the first colon, 'being with the wise–becoming wise', underscored by the repetition of the root *ḥkm*; and in the second colon, 'being with fools–getting into trouble', emphasized by the paronomasia between *rō'eh* and *yērôa'*. The sense connection between *hlwk 't ḥkmym* and *wḥkm* in the first colon, and *wr'h ksylym* and *yrw'* in the second, is reinforced by these repeating sounds. In addition, *hlwk* contributes to the /k/ consonance of colon a and shares a /l, k/ motif with *ksylym* in the second colon.

a. *hālôk 'et ḥ^{a}kāmîm waḥ^{a}kām*	b. *w^{e}rō'eh k^{e}sîlîm yērôa'*
ḥ^{a}kām ḥ^{a}kām	
l k k k	*k l*
	rō' rô '

The paronomasia of the second colon, moreover, underscores the difference between the cola. On the one hand, root repetition in the first colon points toward a highly recommended identity of the wise with their followers. The second colon, on the other hand, while following the pattern of the first in general, uses the wordplay to dramatize a significant difference: this latter companionship (*rō'eh*) is a disaster to be avoided (*yērôa'*). The word *yērôa'* alters the expected parallelism for the second colon: the 'companion of fools' doesn't merely become foolish—he is heading into danger.

Proverbs 11.18. The paronomasia in this proverb is built on a contrast of themes.

a. *rāšā' 'ōśeh p^e'ullat šāqer*	A wicked person makes an empty profit,
b. *w^{e}zōrēa' ṣ^{e}dāqâ śeker '^{e}met*	but the one who sows virtue has a sure reward!

The wordplay joins the noun *šāqer*, used to describe *p^e'ullat* from the first colon, with the noun *śeker* of the second colon. The device, therefore, links both cola, and the way in which *śkr 'mt* echoes *p'lt*

1. This text follows the K. The Q. (*hōlēk . . . yeḥkām*) would work as well for present purposes.

šqr with a /(ś, š), (k, q), r, t/ motif underlines the semantic contrast. The key word *śkr* is also echoed by the /ṣ, q/ motif in *ṣdqh* and *šqr* is echoed by the /r, š/ motif in the first word *rš'*. There is also a sibilant series through most of the proverb.

a. *rš' 'śh p'lt šqr*	b. *wzr' ṣdqh śkr 'mt*
š ś š	*z ṣ ś*
t šqr	*śkr t*
šq	*ṣ q śk*
rš š r	

At the same time, the sound patterns can be viewed in another way—in terms of the parallel phrases. The wordplay between *šqr* and *śkr*, already noted, links the second half of each colon. But the first half of each colon also plays with sounds:

a. *rš' 'śh . . .*	b. *wzr' ṣdqh*
rš' 'ś	*zr' ṣ*

The use of *zr'* provides a phonic link with its opposite partner, the *rš'*, as illustrated above.

Proverbs 12.16. In the next proverb, the words involved in paronomasia are placed next to each other.

a. *'^{e}wîl bayyôm yôdīa'*[1] *ka'sô*	The fool makes his anger known at once;
b. *w^{e}kōseh qālôn 'ārûm*	but the one who is shrewd conceals an injury.

The words *ka'sô* and *kōseh* are certainly not synonyms. But their close proximity in the proverb combined with their obvious consonance does draw attention. In addition, the /ō/ vowel in the last syllable of *ka'sô* and in the first syllable of *kōseh* tightens the wordplay. To be noted here is the use of the *qal* participle of this verb, which is attested mainly in the *piel*. The usage may be explained in part as striving after the paronomastic effect.[2] The juxtaposition of *k'sw* and *ksh* also

1. The MT reads the *niphal* here, *yiwwāda'*, 'is made known', but the versions read the *hiphil*. Either way, the sense is not really changed. The *hiphil* provides a smoother reading and fits in better with the /o/ assonance throughout the saying. Delitzsch (*Biblical Commentary*, VI.1, p. 260), Barucq (*Le livre*, p. 116) and Scott (*Proverbs*, p. 90, n. d) all translate the *hiphil* sense.

2. See p. 94 n. 3. In a similar fashion in Ps. 51.6 the rarer *qal* form *b^{e}dobrekā* is used for assonance with *b^{e}šopṭekā*; see J.S. Kselman, 'A Note on Ps. 51.6', *CBQ* 39 (1977), pp. 251-53.

lines up all /ō/ vowels in a series from *yôm* to *qālôn*. On the basis of sound and position, consequently, the words are closely related.

The two words, *'ᵉwîl* and *'ārûm*, also have a distinct relationship based on their antithetic parallelism. Taking into account, then, the sonant pair *k'sw–ksh* (B, B′) the proverb displays a semantic-sonant chiasmus of the type described by Kselman.[1]

a.	*'wyl* . . .	*k'sw*
	A	B
b.	*wksh* . . .	*'rwm*
	B′	A′

Other sound patterns are the /(k, q)/ consonance in *k'sw, wksh* and *qlwn*, the /i/ assonance between *'ᵉwîl* and *yôdīa'*, and the /'/ consonance in the last words of each colon:

a. *'ᵉwîl bywm ywdīa' k'sw*   b. *wksh qlwn 'rwm*
   î   *ī*
   k   *k q*
   ' '   *'*

Proverbs 13.22. Words rather close in meaning form the wordplay here.

a.	*ṭôb yanḥîl bᵉnê bānîm*	The good man leaves an inheritance for his grandchildren,
b.	*wᵉṣāpûn laṣṣaddîq ḥêl ḥôṭē'*	but the sinner's wealth becomes the just man's treasure.

The alliteration of *ḥêl* in the second colon with *yanḥîl* of the first colon gives these words a clear and ironic association that colors the meaning of each word. The *ḥêl* of the sinner is really not his because he will eventually lose it to the just man. On the other hand, the *ṭwb* (*ṣdyq*) will be able to pass on (*yanḥîl*) not only his own *ḥêl* but the *ḥêl* of the sinner as well. What the proverb is really saying is that the *ṭôb* doubles his inheritance and the *ḥôṭē'* loses all. There is a semantic-sonant chiasmus that links these key words.[2]

1. Kselman, 'Semantic-Sonant Chiasmus', pp. 219-23. This example from Proverbs stretches just a bit the controls for the semantic leg of the chiasmus (as outlined by Kselman, p. 220) to include a fixed pair of antithetic terms.

2. Again, the semantic leg of the chiasmus involves antithetic terms.

a. *ṭwb ynḥyl . . .*
A B

b. *. . . ḥl ḥwṭ'*
B′ A′

The sound patterns found in the proverb echo the association and transactions being described. In the first colon there is a /(b, p), n/ motif that links the *ṭôb* with his *bny bnym* and with the treasure of the *ṣdyq* in the second colon.

a. *ṭwb ynḥyl bny bnym* b. *wṣpwn lṣdyq . . .*
b n bn bn *p n*

The second colon links the just man's treasure with the sinner's wealth by an overlapping /ṣ, l, (d, ṭ)/ motif.

b. *wṣpwn lṣdyq ḥyl ḥwṭ'*
ṣ l d
ṣ l ṭ

With these overlapping phonic structures the proverb links the *ṭwb, bny bnym* and the *ṣdyq* all with the wealth of the sinner, echoing phonically the dispossession that is asserted thematically.

SUMMARY

At this point, after having analysed so many Hebrew proverbs of the OT, it is clear that the assertion with which this study began is unassailable: if sound patterning is characteristic of all poetry, it is likewise characteristic of Hebrew poetry. The examples in Chapter 1, drawn from other ancient and modern languages to demonstrate that assertion, are now paralleled by numerous examples from Hebrew poetry. Although all the examples analysed have been taken from the second part of Proverbs, they represent similar materials found in the broader corpus of OT poetry, as will be clear to anyone familiar with that corpus. It is useful to review what the evidence has shown.

The investigation began in Chapter 2 with the study of various phonic motifs (configurations of repeating sounds). The categories of modern literary criticism were used to describe and systematize the sound patterns of various proverbs. These classifications were only a beginning in the process of understanding these figures of sound and were not intended to be an exclusive means of analysis. Utilizing common phonic patterns produced by assonance, consonance and alliteration, the chapter illustrated their richness and variety and, at the same time, showed how meaning could often be highlighted by such patterns. It also suggested in a few cases the cogency of sound patterns as an opposing or even corroborating argument for textual changes. These latter points continued to be illustrated throughout the rest of the study.

In Chapter 3 linking sound patterns were discussed, that is, sequential phonic links between words and phrases in a proverb, and in Chapter 4, phonic patterns that emphasize the sounds of key words in a proverb. Chapter 5 began a section on tagging sound patterns, those which use phonic motifs to punctuate and mark off syntactical or semantic units in a proverb. Chapter 6 showed how this kind of phonic pattern is often characteristic of proverbs composed of nominal sentences where the predicate echoes the subject. The last chapter collected evidence bearing on the relationship between sound and meaning by studying word repetition and wordplay. All the techniques presented in the previous chapters were brought to bear on the proverbs examined in this final chapter.

This analysis of Hebrew proverbs has left no longer in doubt the question of sound patterning as an integral part of Hebrew poetry. The opinion quoted in the first chapter, namely, that

> there are. . . occasional assonances or rhymes; but these are of irregular occurrence, and obviously do not belong to the essence of the form of the verse,[1]

has no basis in fact. In addition it has made clear that the Hebrew proverbs exploit sound in much the same way as proverbs of other languages and for the same reasons: to please the ear, to attract attention, to make speech worth remembering, to indicate contrast or agreement, and the like. Additional studies of sound patterning in the broader corpus of OT poetry are needed. The techniques of analysis derived from modern literary criticism and employed in this study will hopefully facilitate the effort.

1. Toy, *A Critical Commentary*, p. viii.

BIBLIOGRAPHY

Abel, F.M., *Géographie de la Palestine* (2 vols.; Paris: Gabalda, 1933).

Allison, A.W., *et al.* (eds.), *The Norton Anthology of Poetry* (New York: W.W. Norton, rev. shorter edn, 1975).

Alonso Schökel, L., *Estudios de poética hebrea* (Barcelona: Juan Flors, 1963).

Barucq, A., *Le livre des Proverbes* (SB; Paris: Gabalda, 1964).

Beardslee, W.A., *Literary Criticism of the New Testament* (Philadelphia: Fortress Press, 1970).

—'Uses of the Proverb in the Synoptic Gospels', *Int* 24 (1970), pp. 61-73.

Bergsträsser, E., *Hebräischer Grammatik* (Hildesheim: Georg Olms, 1962).

Berlin, A., *The Dynamics of Biblical Parallelism* (Bloomington, IN: Indiana University Press, 1985).

Bloomfield, L., *Language* (Chicago: University of Chicago Press, repr., 1984).

Boström, G., *Paronomasi i den äldre hebreiska Maschallitteraturen mid särskild Hänsyn till Proverbia* (LUÅ, ns, 1.23, 8: Lund: Gleerup, 1928).

Brooks, C., and R.P. Warren (eds.), *Understanding Poetry* (New York: Holt, Rinehart and Winston, 4th edn, 1976).

Brueggemann, W., 'A Neglected Sapiential Word Pair', *ZAW* 89 (1977), pp. 234-58.

Carlston, C.E., 'Proverbs, Maxims, and the Historical Jesus', *JBL* 99 (1980), pp. 87-105.

Caquot, A., M. Sznycer, and A. Herdner (eds.), *Textes ougaritiques*. I. *Mythes et légendes* (Paris: Cerf, 1974).

Casanowicz, I.M., *Paronomasia in the Old Testament* (Boston: Norwood, 1894).

Ceresko, A.R., 'The Function of Chiasmus in Hebrew Poetry', *CBQ* 40 (1978), pp. 1-10.

Collins, T., *Line-Forms in Hebrew Poetry: A Grammatical Approach to the Stylistic Study of the Hebrew Prophets* (Studia Pohl; Series Maior, 7; Rome: Biblical Institute Press, 1979).

Cooper, A.M., *Biblical Poetics: A Linguistic Approach* (Missoula, MT: Scholars Press, 1979).

Dahood, M., *Proverbs and Northwest Semitic Philology* (Rome: Pontificium Institutum Biblicum, 1963).

—*Psalms* (AB; 3 vols.; New York: Doubleday, 1965–1970).

—'Una coppia di termini ugaritici e Prov 10, 12', *BeO* 15 (1973), pp. 253-54.

Dalman, G., *Arbeit und Sitte in Palästina* (7 vols.; Gütersloh: Bertelsmann, 1928–1942).

Delitzsch, F., *Commentary on the Old Testament*. VI. *Biblical Commentary on the Proverbs of Solomon* (2 parts; trans. J. Martin and M.G. Easton; Grand Rapids, MI: Eerdmans, 1976).

Dietrich, M., O. Loretz and J. Sanmartín, *Die keilalphabetischen Texte aus Ugarit*. I. *Transkription* (AOAT, 24.1; Kevelaer: Verlag Butzon & Bercker; Neukirchen–Vluyn: Neukirchener Verlag, 1976).

Dossin, G., and A. Finet (eds.), *Archives royales de Mari*. X. *Correspondance féminine* (Paris: Librairie Orientaliste Paul Geuthner, 1978).
Driver, G.R., 'Problems in the Hebrew Text of Proverbs', *Bib* 32 (1951), pp. 173-97.
Dundes, A., 'On the Structure of the Proverb', *Proverbium* 25 (1975), pp. 961-73.
Eissfeldt, O., *Der Maschal im Alten Testament* (BZAW, 24; Giessen: Töpelmann, 1913).
Fitzgerald, A., 'A Note on G-Stem *YNṢR* Forms in the Old Testament', *ZAW* 84 (1972), pp. 90-92.
Fogle, S.F., 'Pun', in *Princeton Encyclopedia of Poetry and Poetics* (ed. A. Preminger; Princeton, NJ: Princeton University Press, 1965), pp. 681-82.
—'Repetition', in *Princeton Encyclopedia of Poetry and Poetics* (ed. A. Preminger: Princeton, NJ: Princeton University Press, 1965), pp. 699-701.
Gemser, B., *Sprüche Salomos* (HAT, 16; Tübingen: Mohr [Paul Siebeck], 2nd edn, 1963).
Gibson, J.C.L., *Canaanite Myths and Legends* (Edinburgh: T. & T. Clark, 1977).
Gleason, H.A., Jr, *Linguistics and English Grammar* (New York: Holt, Rinehart and Winston, 1965).
Glück, J.J., 'The Figure of "Inversion" in the Book of Proverbs', *Semitics* 5 (1977), pp. 24-31.
Goldsmith, U.K., 'Alliteration', in *Princeton Encyclopedia of Poetry and Poetics* (ed. A. Preminger; Princeton, NJ: Princeton University Press, 1965), pp. 15-16.
—'Assonance', in *Princeton Encyclopedia of Poetry and Poetics* (ed. A. Preminger; Princeton, NJ: Princeton University Press, 1965), pp. 53-54.
Goldsmith, U.K., and S.L. Mooney, 'Consonance', in *Princeton Encyclopedia of Poetry and Poetics* (ed. A. Preminger; Princeton, NJ: Princeton University Press, 1965), p. 152.
Held, M., 'The *YQTL–QTL (QTL–YQTL)* Sequence of Identical Verbs in Biblical Hebrew and in Ugaritic', in *Studies and Essays in Honor of Abraham A. Neuman* (ed. M. Ben-Horin, B.D. Weinryb and S. Zeitlin; Leiden: Brill, 1962), pp. 281-90.
Hermission, H.-J., *Studien zur israelitischen Spruchweisheit* (WMANT, 28; Neukirchen–Vluyn: Neukirchener Verlag, 1968).
Hobbs, T.R., 'Some Proverbial Reflections in the Book of Jeremiah', *ZAW* 91 (1979), pp. 62-72.
Hoffman, D., 'Proverb', in *Princeton Encyclopedia of Poetry and Poetics* (ed. A. Preminger; Princeton, NJ: Princeton University Press, 1965), p. 680.
Holladay, W.F., 'Form and Word-Play in David's Lament over Saul and Jonathan', *VT* 20 (1970), pp. 153-89.
Jakobson, R., 'Closing Statement: Linguistics and Poetics', in *Style in Language* (ed. T.A. Sebeok; Cambridge, MA: MIT Press, 1975), pp. 350-77.
Jastrow, M., *A Dictionary of the Targumim, the Talmud Babli and Yerushalmi, and the Midrashic Literature* (2 vols.; New York: The Judaica Press, 1975).
Jenni, E., *Das hebräische Pi'el* (Zürich: EVZ-Verlag, 1968).
Johnson, A.R., '*MŠL*', in *Wisdom in Israel and in the Ancient Near East* (ed M. Noth and D.W. Thomas; VTSup, 3; Leiden: Brill, 1960), pp. 162-69.
Joseph, M., *Shakespeare's Use of the Arts of Language* (New York: Columbia University Press, 1947).
Joüon, P., *Grammaire de l'hébreu biblique* (Rome: Pontifical Biblical Institute, corr. photo. edn, 1965).
Kennedy, X.J., *An Introduction to Poetry* (New York: Little, Brown & Co., 1966).

König, F.E., *Historisch-kritisches Lehrgebäude der hebräischen Sprache*. II.2. *Historisch-comparative Syntax der hebräischen Sprache* (Leipzig: Hinrichs, 1897).
Kselman, J.S., 'Semantic-Sonant Chiasmas in Biblical Poetry', *Bib* 58 (1977), pp. 219-23.
—'A Note on Ps. 51.6', *CBQ* 39 (1977), pp. 251-53.
Lagarde, P. de, *Anmerkungen zur griechischen Übersetzung der Proverbien* (Leipzig: Brockhaus, 1863).
Lanham, R.A., *A Handlist of Rhetorical Terms* (Berkeley: University of California Press, 1968).
McKane, W., *Proverbs: A New Approach* (London: SCM Press, 1970).
Mackintosh, R.J. (ed.), *Memoirs of the Life of the Right Honourable Sir James Mackintosh* (2 vols.; London: Edward Moxon, 2nd edn, 1836).
Margalit, B., *A Matter of 'Life' and 'Death': A Study of the Baal-Mot Epic (CTA 4–5–6)* (AOAT, 206; Kevelaer: Butzon & Bercker; Neukirchen–Vluyn: Neukirchener Verlag, 1980).
—'Alliteration in Ugaritic Poetry: Its Rôle in Composition and Analysis', *UF* 11 (1979), pp. 537-57.
Marouzeau, J., *Traité de stylistique appliquée au latin* (Collection d'études latines, Série scientifique, 12; Paris: Société d'Edition, 1935).
Masson, D.I., 'Sound in Poetry', in *Princeton Encyclopedia of Poetry and Poetics* (ed. A. Preminger; Princeton, NJ: Princeton University Press, 1965), pp. 784-89.
—'Thematic Analysis of Sounds in Poetry', in *Essays on the Language of Literature* (ed. S. Chatman and S.R. Levin; Boston: Houghton Mifflin, 1967), pp. 54-68.
—'Vowel and Consonant Patterns in Poetry', in *Essays on the Language of Literature* (ed. S. Chatman and S.R. Levin; Boston: Houghton Mifflin, 1967), pp. 3-18.
Melamed, E.Z., 'Break-Up of Stereotype Phrases as an Artistic Device in Biblical Poetry', *Scripta Hierosolymitana* 8 (1961), pp. 115-53.
Miller, P.D., '*YĀPÎAḤ* in Psalm xii 6', *VT* 29 (1979), pp. 495-501.
Murphy, R.E., 'Form Criticism and Wisdom Literature', *CBQ* 31 (1969), pp. 475-83.
—'The Kerygma of the Book of Proverbs', *Int* 20 (1966), pp. 3-14.
O'Connor, M., *Hebrew Verse Structure* (Winona Lake, IN: Eisenbrauns, 1979).
—'The Rhetoric of the Kilamuwa Inscription', *BASOR* 226 (1977), pp. 15-29.
Oesterley, W.O.E., *The Book of Proverbs* (New York: E.P. Dutton, 1929).
Pardee, D., '*YPḤ* "Witness" in Hebrew and Ugaritic', *VT* 28 (1978), pp. 204-13.
Payne, D.F., 'A Perspective on the Use of Simile in the Old Testament', *Semitics* 1 (1970), pp. 111-25.
Perdue, L.G., *Wisdom and Cult* (SBLDS, 30; Missoula, MT: Scholars Press, 1977).
Perrine, L., *Sound and Sense* (New York: Harcourt Brace Jovanovich, 4th edn, 1973).
Ploeg, J. van der, 'Prov xxv 23', *VT* 3 (1953), pp. 189-91.
Priebatsch, H.Y., 'Spiranten und Aspiratae in Ugarit, AT und Hellas', *UF* 12 (1980), pp. 317-33.
Rad, G. von, *Old Testament Theology*. I. *The Theology of Israel's Historical Traditions* (trans. D.M.G. Stalker; New York: Harper & Row, 1962).
—*Wisdom in Israel* (trans. J.D. Martin; Nashville: Abingdon Press, 1977).
Ringgren, H., and W. Zimmerli, *Sprüche. Prediger* (ATD, 16.1; Göttingen: Vandenhoeck & Ruprecht, 1962).
Robert, A., 'Le Yahvisme de Prov x, 1–xxii, 16; xxv–xxix', in *Mémorial Lagrange* (Paris: Gabalda, 1940), pp. 163-82.

Robertson, D.A., *Linguistic Evidence in Dating Early Hebrew Poetry* (SBLDS, 3; Missoula, MT: Scholars Press, 1972).
Scott, R.B.Y., *Proverbs, Ecclesiastes* (AB, 18; Garden City, NY: Doubleday, 1965).
—*The Way of Wisdom in the Old Testament* (New York: Macmillan, 1971).
Shipley, J.T. (ed.), *Dictionary of World Literary Terms* (Boston: The Writer, rev. and enlarged edn, 1970).
Skladny, U., *Die ältesten Spruchsammlungen in Israel* (Göttingen: Vandenhoeck & Ruprecht, 1962).
Stevenson, B. (ed.), *The Home Book of Proverbs, Maxims and Familiar Phrases* (New York: Macmillan, 1948).
Strus, A., 'La poétique sonore des récits de la Genèse', *Bib* 60 (1979), pp. 1-22.
Taylor, A., *The Proverb* (Cambridge, MA: Harvard University Press, 1931).
Thomas, D.W., 'Some Passages in the Book of Proverbs', in *Wisdom in Israel and in the Ancient Near East* (ed. M. Noth and D.W. Thomas; VTSup, 3; Leiden: Brill, 1960), pp. 280-92.
Thompson, J.M., *The Form and Function of Proverbs in Ancient Israel* (The Hague: Mouton, 1974).
Tromp, N.J., *Primitive Conceptions of Death and the Nether World in the Old Testament* (BibOr, 21; Rome: Pontifical Biblical Institute, 1969).
Toy, C.H., *A Critical and Exegetical Commentary on the Book of Proverbs* (ICC; Edinburgh: T. & T. Clark, 1970).
Ullmann, S., *Language and Style* (Oxford: Basil Blackwell, 1964).
Untermeyer, L. (ed.), *Complete Poems of Edgar Allen Poe* (New York: The Hermitage Press, 1943).
Weiden, W.A. van der, '"Abstractum pro concreto", phaenomenon stilisticum', *VD* 44 (1966), pp. 43-52.
—*Le livre des Proverbes: Notes philologiques* (BibOr, 23; Rome: Biblical Institute Press, 1970).
Wilkinson, L.P., *Golden Latin Artistry* (Cambridge: Cambridge University Press, 1963).
Zimmerli, W., 'Zur Struktur der alttestamentlichen Weisheit', *ZAW* 51 (1953), pp. 177-204.
Zorell, F., *Lexicon hebraicum et aramaicum Veteris Testamenti* (Rome: Pontificium Institutum Biblicum, 1954).

INDEXES

INDEX OF BIBLICAL REFERENCES

Genesis
2.7 121
3.19 121
9.6 76
27.36 76
37.35 69

Numbers
16.33 69

Deuteronomy
28.13-14 69

Joshua
11.4 133

1 Samuel
2.3 104
17.7 128

2 Samuel
19.1 128

1 Kings
18.43-45 115

2 Kings
9.23 91

Isaiah
5.6 132
7.23 132
7.24 132
7.25 132
9.17 132
28.10 84
28.13 84
29.8 116
53.9 91
55.10 121
59.7 132
60.18 132
62.3 132

Jeremiah
13.18 132
17.11 107
52.20 128

Ezekiel
10.3 127
16.12 132
16.63 104
23.42 132
29.21 104

Hosea
12.9 140

Amos
4.1 140
5.11-12 140
6.4-7 140
8.5 91
8.6 140

Micah
6.12 140
7.5 104

Zechariah
9.10 133

Psalms
16.9-11 69
22.9 34
32.1 94
37.5 34
40.12 36
49.12 140
49.20 140
51.5-7 74
51.6 151
55.16 69
61.8 36
73.24 69
90.3 121
122.9 87
141.3 104
143.6 116

Job
1.9-11 121
1.21 121
15.16 80
20.10 140
20.12-15 80
21.23-26 140
22.7 116
27.16-17 140

Proverbs
1.20 41
4.9 132
6.1 145
10.1 131
10.5 126
10.9 122, 124
10.12 31
10.14 96
10.17 33
10.26 76
11.1 91
11.2 16
11.4 59
11.6 140
11.7 138, 140

11.8 140
11.10 77
11.13 33, 93, 94
11.15 145
11.18 150
11.21 55
11.22 108
11.26 65
12.1 101, 102
12.5 36, 91
12.6 107
12.8 34
12.11 130
12.16 94, 151
12.17 91
12.23 94
12.25 40, 41
13.3 33, 96, 98
13.4 126
13.6 39, 40
13.7 33
13.13 102
13.20 150
13.22 140, 152
13.24 105
14.5 144
14.13 128
14.23 56
15.8 83
15.12 21, 46, 47
15.24 13, 68, 69
15.27 143
15.28 80
15.29 55
15.31 52
15.32 21, 95
16.3 34
16.10 67
16.17 98
16.23 78
16.26 145
16.31 60, 61, 132
17.3 109-112
17.6 132
17.8 54
17.15 142
17.18 144
17.19 103
17.25 81
18.3 122, 125
18.7 96
18.13 32
19.5 42, 43
19.8 100
19.9 43
19.16 102
19.17 65
19.26 82
19.28 79
20.6 129
20.9 74
20.18 35, 91
20.19 92-94, 96, 100, 101, 103, 135, 143
20.28 36
21.5 57, 91
21.8 13, 58
21.17 135
21.21 37
21.23 104
21.24 67
21.30 134
22.7 66
22.10 61
22.13 84
22.22-23 146, 147
22.29 136
23.1-3 48-50
24.3-4 72, 73
24.7 104
24.19-20 147, 148
24.29 140
25.11 112, 114
25.12 113
25.13 71
25.23 114
25.25 116
25.28 47
26.3 117
26.13 84
26.14 118
27.8 133
27.14 43
27.19 122
27.21 109-112
28.19 130
29.7 146
29.10 85
29.12 54

Ecclesiastes
3.15 87
3.19-20 140
3.21 69
9.2-5 140

Esther
7.7 87

Nehemiah
2.10 87

Sirach
8.8 137
38.3 137
39.4 137
50.27 112

Luke
12.54 115

INDEX OF AUTHORS

Abel, F.M. 115
Allison, A.W. 20
Alonso Schökel, L. 13
Barucq, A. 40, 69, 72, 87, 102, 112, 123, 125, 129, 140, 151
Beardslee, W.A. 14
Bergsträsser, G. 100
Berlin, A. 12
Bloomfield, L. 14
Boström, G. 11, 13, 33-35, 38, 41-46, 48, 58, 66, 70, 71, 73, 77, 80-82, 86, 87, 95-97, 99, 100-102, 104, 105, 107-109, 112, 114, 116-18, 137, 147
Brooks, C. 24, 29, 120
Browning, E.B. 120
Brueggemann, W. 125
Carlston, C.E. 14
Casanowicz, I.M. 13, 25
Ceresko, A.R. 73
Cervantes, M. de 15
Coleridge, S.T. 30
Collins, T. 12
Cooper, A.M. 12
Dahood, M. 31, 40, 50, 102
Dalman, G. 115
Delitzsch, F. 44, 45, 48, 57, 80, 81, 86, 107, 112, 125, 139, 151
Dickinson, E. 27
Dietrich, M. 18
Donne, J. 26, 29
Dossin, G. 15
Driver, G.R. 58, 63
Dundes, A. 15
Ennius 21
Finet, A. 15
Fitzgerald, A. 96
Fogle, S.F. 120, 149
Frankenberg, W. 80
Frost, R. 29
Gemser, B. 36, 38, 39, 44, 58, 70, 72, 80, 84, 85, 87, 102, 104, 112, 125, 129, 137, 139
Gleason, H.A. Jr 14
Glück, J.J. 127
Goldsmith, U.K. 26-28
Held, M. 139
Hermisson, H.-J. 11, 33, 98, 104, 107
Hobbs, T.R. 14
Holladay, W.F. 52
Hopkins, G.M. 20, 64
Housman, A.E. 20, 65
Jakobson, R. 12, 13, 25, 52
Jastrow, M. 35
Jenni, E. 94
Joseph, M. 149
Joüon, P. 20, 41, 94, 100, 107, 111, 128
Keats, J. 25, 30
Kennedy, X.J. 28
König, F.E. 40, 128
Kselman, J. 76, 79, 151, 152
Lagarde, P. de 63
Lanham, R.A. 28
Loretz, O. 18
Lowell, R. 29
Lucretius 18
McKane, W. 11, 38, 41, 69, 84, 112, 123, 125, 129
Mackintosh, R.J. 15
Margalit, B. 19
Marouzeau, J. 18-21
Masson, D.I. 12, 22, 25, 29, 30, 52, 64, 75

Melamed, E.Z. 133
Miller, P.D. 43
Mooney, S.L. 26
Murphy, R.E. 14
O'Connor, M. 12, 17
Oesterley, W.O.E. 139
Owen, W. 75
Pardee, D. 43
Payne, D.F. 109
Perdue, L.G. 83
Perrine, L. 28
Plautus 20
Ploeg, J. van der 115
Poe, E.A. 25
Pope, A. 24
Prietbatsch, H.Y. 32
Rad, G. von 16
Ringgren, H. 38, 39, 80, 125, 137, 139
Robert, A. 69
Robertson, D.A. 41, 42
Russell, J. 15
Sanmartín, J. 18
Scott, R.B.Y. 37, 41, 44, 45, 58, 80, 85, 89, 123, 125, 138, 151
Shakespeare, W. 88, 149, 150
Shipley, J.T. 88
Skladny, U. 11
Stevenson, B. 15, 51
Strus, A. 76
Taylor, A. 15
Thomas, D.W. 83
Thompson, J.M. 14
Tromp, N.J. 80
Toy, C.H. 13, 36, 37, 40, 41, 44, 48, 54, 72, 80, 83, 86, 102, 108, 112, 114, 115, 125, 129, 139, 155
Ullmann, S. 106
Untermeyer, L. 25
Virgil 18, 19
Warren, R.P. 24, 29, 120
Weiden, W.A. van der 36, 40, 83
Whitman, W. 120
Wilkinson, L.P. 18
Zimmerli, W. 11, 38
Zorell, F. 40, 87

JOURNAL FOR THE STUDY OF THE OLD TESTAMENT

Supplement Series

65 THERE IS HOPE FOR A TREE:
THE TREE AS METAPHOR IN ISAIAH
K. Nielsen
66 SECRETS OF THE TIMES:
MYTH AND HISTORY IN BIBLICAL CHRONOLOGY
J. Hughes
67 ASCRIBE TO THE LORD:
BIBLICAL AND OTHER ESSAYS IN MEMORY OF PETER C. CRAIGIE
Edited by L. Eslinger & G. Taylor
68 THE TRIUMPH OF IRONY IN THE BOOK OF JUDGES
L.R. Klein
69 ZEPHANIAH, A PROPHETIC DRAMA
P.R. HOUSE
70 NARRATIVE ART IN THE BIBLE
S. Bar-Efrat
71 QOHELET AND HIS CONTRADICTIONS
M.V. Fox
73 DAVID'S SOCIAL DRAMA:
A HOLOGRAM OF THE EARLY IRON AGE
J.W. Flanagan
74 THE STRUCTURAL ANALYSIS OF BIBLICAL AND CANAANITE POETRY
Edited by W. van der Meer & J.C. de Moor
75 DAVID IN LOVE AND WAR:
THE PURSUIT OF POWER IN 2 SAMUEL 10–12
R.C. Bailey
76 GOD IS KING:
UNDERSTANDING AN ISRAELITE METAPHOR
M. Brettler
77 EDOM AND THE EDOMITES
J.R. Bartlett
78 SWALLOWING THE SCROLL:
TEXTUALITY AND THE DYNAMICS OF DISCOURSE IN EZEKIEL'S PROPHECY
E.F. Davies
79 GIBEAH: THE SEARCH FOR A BIBLICAL CITY
P.M. Arnold
80 THE NATHAN NARRATIVES
G.H. Jones
81 ANTI-COVENANT:
COUNTER-READING WOMEN'S LIVES IN THE HEBREW BIBLE
Edited by M. Bal

82 RHETORIC AND BIBLICAL INTERPRETATION
D. Patrick & A. Scult
83 THE EARTH AND THE WATERS IN GENESIS 1 AND 2
D.T. Tsumura
84 INTO THE HANDS OF THE LIVING GOD
L. Eslinger
85 FROM CARMEL TO HOREB: ELIJAH IN CRISIS
A.J. Hauser & R. Gregory
86 THE SYNTAX OF THE VERB IN CLASSICAL HEBREW PROSE
A. Niccacci
87 THE BIBLE IN THREE DIMENSIONS
Edited by D.J.A. Clines, S.E. Fowl & S.E. Porter
88 THE PERSUASIVE APPEAL OF THE CHRONICLER:
A RHETORICAL ANALYSIS
R.K. Duke
89 THE PROBLEM OF THE PROCESS OF TRANSMISSION
IN THE PENTATEUCH
R. Rendtorff
90 BIBLICAL HEBREW IN TRANSITION:
THE LANGUAGE OF THE BOOK OF EZEKIEL
M.F. Rooker
91 THE IDEOLOGY OF RITUAL:
SPACE, TIME, AND STATUS IN THE PRIESTLY THEOLOGY
F.H. Gorman
92 ON HUMOUR AND THE COMIC IN THE HEBREW BIBLE
Edited by Y.T. Radday & A. Brenner
93 JOSHUA 24 AS POETIC NARRATIVE
W.T. Koopmans
94 WHAT DOES EVE DO TO HELP? AND OTHER READERLY QUESTIONS
TO THE OLD TESTAMENT
D.J.A. Clines
95 GOD SAVES: LESSONS FROM THE ELISHA STORIES
R.D. Moore
96 ANNOUNCEMENTS OF PLOT IN GENESIS
L.A. Turner
97 THE UNITY OF THE TWELVE
P.R. House
98 ANCIENT CONQUEST ACCOUNTS: A STUDY IN ANCIENT NEAR
EASTERN AND BIBLICAL HISTORY WRITING
K. Lawson Younger, Jr
99 WEALTH AND POVERTY IN THE BOOK OF PROVERBS
R.N. Whybray
100 A TRIBUTE TO GEZA VERMES. ESSAYS ON JEWISH AND CHRISTIAN
LITERATURE AND HISTORY
Edited by P.R. Davies & R.T. White

101 THE CHRONICLER IN HIS AGE
P.R. Ackroyd
102 THE PRAYERS OF DAVID (PSALMS 51–72)
M.D. Goulder
103 THE SOCIOLOGY OF POTTERY IN ANCIENT PALESTINE:
THE CERAMIC INDUSTRY AND THE DIFFUSION OF CERAMIC STYLE
IN THE BRONZE AND IRON AGES
Bryant G. Wood
104 PSALM-STRUCTURES:
A STUDY OF PSALMS WITH REFRAINS
Paul R. Raabe
107 THE ALIEN IN THE PENTATEUCH
Christiana van Houten
108 THE FORGING OF ISRAEL:
IRON TECHNOLOGY, SYMBOLISM AND TRADITION IN
ANCIENT SOCIETY
Paula McNutt
109 SCRIBES AND SCHOOLS IN MONARCHIC JUDAH
David Jamieson-Drake
110 THE CANAANITES AND THEIR LAND:
THE TRADITION OF THE CANAANITES
Niels Peter Lemche
112 WISDOM IN REVOLT:
METAPHORICAL THEOLOGY IN THE BOOK OF JOB
Leo G. Perdue
113 PROPERTY AND THE FAMILY IN BIBLICAL LAW
Raymond Westbrook
114 A TRADITIONAL QUEST:
ESSAYS IN HONOUR OF LOUIS JACOBS
Edited by Dan Cohn-Sherbok
116 NARRATIVE AND NOVELLA IN SAMUEL:
STUDIES BY HUGO GRESSMANN AND OTHER SCHOLARS 1906-1923
Edited by David M. Gunn
117 SECOND TEMPLE STUDIES
Edited by P.R. Davies
118 SEEING AND HEARING GOD WITH THE PSALMS:
PROPHETIC LITURGY FROM THE SECOND TEMPLE IN JERUSALEM
R.J. Tournay
119 TELLING QUEEN MICHAL'S STORY:
AN EXPERIMENT IN COMPARATIVE INTERPRETATION
Edited by David J.A. Clines & Tamara C. Eskenazi
120 THE REFORMING KINGS:
CULT AND SOCIETY IN FIRST TEMPLE JUDAH
Richard H. Lowery

121 KING SAUL IN THE HISTORIOGRAPHY OF JUDAH
Diana Vikander Edelman

122 IMAGES OF EMPIRE
Edited by Loveday Alexander

124 LAW AND IDEOLOGY IN MONARCHIC ISRAEL
Edited by Baruch Halpern and Deborah W. Hobson

125 PRIESTHOOD AND CULT IN ANCIENT ISRAEL
Edited by Gary A. Anderson and Saul M. Olyan

127 THE FABRIC OF HISTORY:
TEXT, ARTIFACT AND ISRAEL'S PAST
Edited by Diana Vikander Edelman

131 FORMS OF DEFORMITY: A MOTIF-INDEX OF ABNORMALITIES, DEFORMITIES AND DISABILITIES IN TRADITIONAL JEWISH LITERATURE
Lynn Holden